BEING MAMA

Charleyne Oulton, Deirdre Slattery, Erica Lambert,
Habiba Jessica Zaman, Liz Vardan,
Samantha Amaraegbu, Jenna Knight, Sasha Rose,
Sarah MacElroy, Shannon-Lee Figsby, Valerie Steele

GOLDEN BRICK ROAD
PUBLISHING HOUSE

Published in Canada, for Global Distribution by Golden Brick Road Publishing House Inc.

www.goldenbrickroad.pub

For more information email: kylee@gbrph.ca

ISBN: 9781988736679

To order additional copies of this book: orders@gbrph.ca

Contents

Nurtured Mama

Driven Mama

Forever Mama

Introduction

We juggle a lot of things at once that each resemble a boulder made of glass: fragile and heavy. Emotions, job expectations, finances, relationships, health, and for some there's also medically compromised children or family members, family separation and divorce, and running a business. With all that we do comes labels and titles, we are known as; girl, her, she, Miss, friend, girlfriend; and we become a woman, partner, Mrs., wife, widow, divorcee, bosswoman, career woman, home owner, and the big one—Mom. Being a mama takes on many more subtitles such as: chauffeur, maid, laundromat attendee, pet sitter, moments of being your kid's best friend and confidant, but also moments of being the worst-friend-ever, ruler, boss, alarm-clock, "meanie," costume designer, gift wrapper, personal shopper, medical caregiver, tucker-inner, protector from monsters under the bed, and so much more.

As women, in our many roles in career and life, with all the subsidiary tasks they each include, we need to take time to tell our story, to build our story, and to live it. How has being mama shifted and impacted your life as a woman, as a human being? We have similarities in our journeys, but also some things one mama-bear might experience, we could never imagine.

Being Mama: A Real Look at the Roller Coaster of Motherhood: Struggle, Strength, Passion and Love, is a book to share all kinds of stories about the different experiences of motherhood and womanhood. How does one embrace motherhood while still being herself? When mama is the be-all to her littles, how does she adapt and keep her cool with being a new mama, or being a driven mama? What can she do to set aside time for herself? When she is a strong support to many, who supports her?

Our authors have found communities, have pursued passions and careers, health and body image, and creative outlets (such as making the leap into authorship), but it was a juggling act. When fulfilling many titles, there is compromise and sacrifice. There are times when keeping your head above water is downright challenging. Expressing and relating to others has always been key in processing and growth, so that is what we aim to do here with this book. Dive into our stories and feel less alone within your own. Laugh, cry, be inspired, think, and reach out to us. We are putting ourselves out there to build a village; to ask for support and be supportive.

We ask you to celebrate your wins and the wins of other mamas, to be a soundboard if a fellow mama needs that or to simply have an adult conversation with her. Don't we all want the same things? Enjoyment, health, career, and a hobby? Being mama is the hardest title, but also rewarding beyond what many can imagine. So mama, it's time to take time for YOU. Kick up your feet, tell them mama time is important too, and find some new friends within these pages.

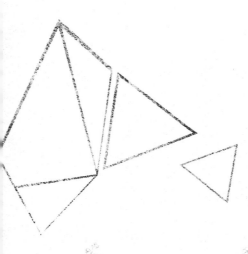

BEING MAMA

Welcome to motherhood.
You sleep like shit.
Feel like shit.
Tired of everybody's shit.
But you love those little shits.

@fruitsofmotherhood

Nurtured Mama

Section 1

Featuring:
Deirdre Slattery
Charleyne Oulton
Liz Vardan

New outfit
Undress with confidence
Run a bath
Turn in early
Uncork some wine
Read a book
Eat the cake
Dance with your children

Being a nurtured mama is being a woman who is cared for while she cares for others. Whether that be receiving help from her family, her partner, her children, or herself. To nurture is to care for, and encourage growth and development; that is exactly what mama's do for their littles on a daily basis, isn't it? But what about nurturing herself? These mama's have found a way to love themselves and share that love with their children. Dive in and see how simply sharing a meal with your child, sharing a new exercise, or sharing your new found health knowledge with your growing children can help them through life. Trust me, I know how hard it is to take an hour for yourself to hit the gym, to hop in the bath, maybe have a date night with your loved one, or just to be by yourself! Guilt is a big part of motherhood, and we are here to share with you, through this insane journey of raising littles, that it is OK to desire time for yourself. Now it's time to put that desire into action and do something for YOU!

Mama, please find something that makes YOU smile, and nurture your body and soul so you can nurture your children. Maybe they will learn a thing or two, and will help nurture you as well!

Chapter One

Fit Mama, Fit (Healthy) Family

"The best gifts I can offer as a mom are my lessons learned and the example I lead by. There is only one option when you see the eyes of your child watching and rooting for you, to live your best and never give up."

Deirdre Slattery

www.deirdreslattery_arbonne.com

ig: @deirdre_sfitness | fb: @fitandfabpreneur

Deirdre Slattery

Deirdre is a single mother to a beautiful daughter who is her greatest support, and who has brought out her passions to be her best; a healthy, positive, and strong independent woman. Deirdre sees change as a constant opportunity to learn, grow, and make the best of life around her. She is an eternal optimist with grounded and practical balance. This free spirit has spent time travelling the globe and learning about life and feels most at home near the water with people who are living healthy, thriving, and being happy. Helping others to see their potential comes naturally to Deirdre, and finding the good in every situation makes her life's work meaningful. Her purpose is to inspire and motivate others to stay positive and strong in any adversity.

Deirdre received a bachelor's of kinesiology and education from the University of Windsor and majored in biology and health education. She is a three-time best-selling author and an award-winning fitness model. After twenty years, she is following her heart to expand her career by sharing tools to help people become the best version of themselves. Her entrepreneurial plans include making a greater impact in the health and fitness industry, and lifestyle coaching. She finds the most reward in helping others unlock and overcome their barriers to live the life of their dreams. She is open-minded and open-hearted, and there to listen and guide others to their best in health and wellness.

There is a surreal moment shared by all first time mamas—that moment when it's just you and your baby for the first time. When I experienced this moment, I heard doubt in my head; *I am being left on my own to raise this child?* The fear, anxiety, and excitement can be overwhelming and daunting. All the prenatal, expecting prep books in the world cannot prepare you for this total transformation in body, mind, and spirit.

I had to come to terms with being a mom and taking care of not only my child, but also myself. *How can we do it all?* As a fitness coach and lifestyle consultant, the most common question I am asked by moms is, "how can I find the time to get fit?" This question often comes with a load of guilt for taking time away from family to work on themselves. However, the other side of this is beautiful. Once they find a way to put their health on the map and a way to place themselves on the top of the list, a more vibrant, happy, and calm mama shows up! And the fan club— their children and partner—is there proudly cheering them on.

To get started, I encourage you to sit with yourself for a moment, take a deep breath, look into your mind and locate your *why.* That one thing that lights you up, gets you out of bed in the morning, puts one foot in front of the other. Your *why* will make your wish to be healthier, more personal and meaningful, and give you the push you need to make informed decisions. *Is your why your children?* If so, you might feel guilty about taking time for your own fitness. *Did your priorities shift when you became a parent?* But taking care of yourself first is not selfish; it is imperative to your overall health. Without a healthy mama, mentally and physically, what is left? We are constantly modeling all we do with our best intentions and our children are watching and soaking up all they see.

We work so hard and deserve to pause in the moment, take a deep breath, and acknowledge and appreciate all we have been doing. There is no perfect recipe for success or a foolproof plan to help us be the best at it all. With the next breath forgive yourself for everything you have relentlessly blamed yourself, criticized yourself, and beaten yourself up for. Let it go and let in what you need to read, hear, or think to shift in your mindset to be better to yourself. This will only help you to become better for the little ones depending on you. Leave that guilt at the door, Mama!

My mission as a new mom was to give my daughter fresh, homemade, healthy food, foster her creativity, and build a foundation for a healthy, active lifestyle that would make her happy and confident in her body and mind. All the prep work, grocery shopping, cooking, cleaning, running to parent-and-toddler swim, music, playdates, and library visits somehow had me feeling like I was in the ultimate race of my life. My days consisted of having a difficult time saying goodbye at daycare, arriving at work, rushing to pick-up time, doing homework (eventually), dinner time, play time, bedtime routines, and then trying to stay awake for *me* time, whether that was work or leisure. I went from being very fit and healthy to feeling very tired and worn out. My only consistent exercise was cleaning, stroller walks, and lugging a car seat and groceries into the house. I lacked balance and time to do it all. The gym and my recreational sports seemed to be the first things to get cut when my stress and other demands were high. The more I set my sports and gym life aside, the more I felt isolated and knew I was not living my life to my fullest. The longer I stayed away from the gym, the less willpower I had to take care of my own health. When working with my clients, it became, "do as I say, not as I do."

I went through sprints and there were crash-and-burns along the way. Every year, I would set goals to get in shape for spring break, summer, or a season, but I didn't have the commitment or passion to keep going without extended breaks and fluctuations in my overall fitness level and energy levels. This off-again, on-again pattern lasted for many years. I was trying to do a lot and not feeling like I was doing particularly well at any of it, now, I can see the gap. The gap between what I knew I needed to do for my body and what I was actually doing. To close this gap, I needed to be unapologetic when taking care of myself for myself.

I hit a point in my life as a single mom when I was working full time and my relationships seemed to constantly not work out. After several difficult breakups, I was feeling very low and dissatisfied with myself, and couldn't see the way to make it better. I didn't believe in myself enough or think I was truly worthy and capable of better. *Why do we deem ourselves unworthy any time things get a little tough?* I hope that all the moms reading this can start to see their worth, always, and work to guard it. Realize it, own it, and embrace it before you hit that place of worthlessness that I did. Being a mama is an incredible gift, and we have a duty to honor ourselves, and foster and nurture healthy children in every way.

So what is my *why,* you ask? To start at day one in the next chapter of my life, to find a lasting way to better my overall health, and to rise up and be strong in body, mind, and spirit for my daughter and myself.

Having a clear vision for your life, with goals and a deeply rooted *why,* will make a great foundation for your plan to live your best life. When it comes to health goals, I recommend making a total shift from the attitude of one day, someday, to the attitude of today is the day, day one. Now is the only moment we all have. I have learned from experience how much of my day *I* control with the choices I make from the second I wake till the moment I fall asleep.

We make approximately 35,000 conscious decisions a day, and 226.7 of them involve food.[1] With that number of decisions in a day, it's no wonder fatigue sets in when we're home from a long day at work. This fatigue can make the decision about whether or not to workout so difficult. Here are a few suggestions that may get you motivated.

- Hire a personal trainer. They can provide the willpower and strength needed to beat your biggest excuses and push you past your comfort zone.
- Be prepared with set workout times, dates with a workout buddy, your gym clothes in the car, and ample nutritious food and water, to give you the energy to train and be fully hydrated.
- Plan your day, week, and month. Booking training sessions and plan menus. I find Sundays are a great day to set up my week and clear the time and space in my calendar. Make sure to **keep those dates with yourself.** Keeping your word will build your integrity, internal motivation, and willpower.
- Become a morning club goer! Get your *you-time* in before your children (and the majority of people) wake up for the day.
- Get your beauty and "bootie" sleep. Sleep helps your mind be fresh for the day, and your body needs sleep to build and repair muscles.

---

1   Graff, Frank. February 7, 2018. "How many daily decisions do we make?" http://science.unctv.org/content/reportersblog/choices

My own transformation started with the desire to be healthy and feel good in my own body. For most of my life as a mom, my focus on being *in shape* had me feeling tired, depressed, weak, and broken down. Then my shift happened, and I realized that in order to care for others, I needed to take care of myself first. I wanted to move past that, to a place I had only dreamed of, but never had the courage to strive to reach. I was almost forty-four and hired a personal trainer, established a meal plan that helped me to eat regularly (low fat, low carb, high protein, and lots of water, vitamins, and minerals), and lowered my intake of added sugar, alcohol, and unhealthy fats. I made a goal, found the right people to help me stay accountable, and I worked on both my physical and my mental health to prove to myself and my daughter that I am strong, capable, and worthy of feeling healthy, vibrant, and confident. It was a conscious decision put into action the moment I declared it and shared it, I made myself responsible and accountable to myself, my trainer, my daughter, and my friends and family. I was coming up on my forty-fourth birthday, and my goal was to feel the best I could on *that day.*

My workouts were hard in the beginning, but my big goal, and the knowledge that my daughter's eyes were on me, kept me committed. Every workout was a release of tears and negative energy, and my thoughts until my inner voice started to say, *I can and I will.* I felt a change, from dragging myself around and feeling low and depleted, to feeling genuinely happy to get dressed and ready to go. My workouts became more vigorous and empowering, and I came home feeling like I could handle anything in front of me. Each workout built another layer of strength and confidence in myself and gave me the courage to overcome any obstacle in my way.

I fell in love with the gift of being able to move my body, and train my brain to be stronger and more resilient to unforeseen changes and things out of my control. The body is a remarkable

21

home, and I cherish what it allows me to do in a day, from walking, to running, to working out, to having the energy for my job as a mom, and to my work with clients. Many of my clients are hard-working mamas who have also chosen to give themselves the time to care for their bodies.They have made the choice to better their physical strength while developing positive self-esteem and body image. When we constantly fill our own cup, we can lift our level of self-worth and improve our capacity to give back to our families and the rest of the world.

I urge new moms to enjoy and cherish the newborns and toddlers, the precious moments, because time does seem to pass quickly. Find time to take care of yourself, too, however that works for you. Include your child in your activity and make it fun to begin fostering a healthy active lifestyle early on.

And for myself, I have a teenager now. The dynamics change as our children grow; I have the freedom and flexibility to plan a lot of my workouts around her schedule now. When I can't, she is my biggest cheerleader for self-care. She sees the results in my overall health and happiness when I constantly work out. Letting go of the guilt for putting yourself first sometimes is imperative for better overall health. Exercise releases endorphins, the feel-good hormone that will keep you going back. It can also help ward off the blues we all feel from time to time, and for some, like myself, it can help get us through depression and anxiety. How we feel on the inside will shine outward, and of course, the physical outer shell will benefit from all the hard work.

Since that decision to make my life the best it can be, I have changed my career. I am now a self-employed transformational coach, training others in fitness and health. I have been published in six magazines as a fitness model, won my first fitness competition, became an award-winning co-author published in four books, and led my first co-author book, which became a best-seller. I continue to evolve and take on new challenges. This journey has inspired me to help others and find my own true passions and calling. I have one beautiful human watching me and believing in me, in everything I do. I have a responsibility to her to be the best version of myself. I want to demonstrate that health is not only what we choose to feed our families; it is the lifestyle we create for them. By being healthy ourselves, we'll be better able to give our children strategies to manage life stressors, confidence to go for their dreams and to take action daily, and to live life to the fullest—body, mind, and spirit.

Chapter Two

Spread Love for Food Like Peanut Butter on Warm Bread

"I want my children to have a love and appreciation for food as big as my love for peanut butter."

Charleyne Oulton

www.coachcharleybrown.com

ig: coach.charley.brown | fb: coachcharleybrown
Portraiture by: Katie Jean Photography, Mill Bay, BC

Charleyne Oulton

Charleyne Oulton has a passion for plant-based nutrition and a desire to make healthy eating an easy, fast, tasty, and a fun habit for herself and her young family. She is a confident, happy, divorced mom of three who lives on beautiful Vancouver Island, BC, Canada.

She is a celebrated award-winning author published through Golden Brick Road Publishing House in: *Dear Time*, *Are You on My Side?*, *On Her Plate*, *Her Art of Surrender*, and the original *You've Got This Mama, Too*. Charleyne loves to share her personal health journey with the world and is an established health and wellness coach with It Works Global. She is also an active reserve member of the Royal Canadian Navy, currently attached to The Naval Security Team.

airy Cow

"Swoosh, swoosh, swoosh" came the dull hum of the electric breast pump. I will never forget that feeling, like I was glued to this beast. In this chapter of my life, I felt like I had somehow switched lives with an actual dairy cow. On a few occasions, our freezer had no room for any food, or even ice cube trays, because it was filled with packets and bottles of breast milk. I remember feeling so proud of myself but also so frustrated because we were running out of room to store my milk. As a solution we purchased a small deep freezer, this was a great solution, until it also became full.

My three children were born very premature, and all within three years and three months of each other. Jaiden was born at thirty-two weeks gestation and weighed five pounds, Jeffrie was born at almost twenty-eight weeks gestation and weighed less than three pounds, and Juley-Anne was born at twenty-six weeks gestation and weighed a mere two pounds. Their tiny bodies needed my *liquid gold*, but pumping it round the clock was not an easy task. I had to pump every three hours, through the night, even while pregnant, to keep my milk supply up and nourish my little loves, all while juggling new mom life, recovering from surgery, and sitting down to feed my babies. If you are a mother, you may agree that personal health and self-care take a backseat as you find yourself caring for everyone else around you. This is exactly what happened to me. My only focus and concern during this stage of life was taking care of my little loves. I am proud to say I pumped and nursed for a grand total of twenty-nine months, straight. Through pregnancy, cracked nipples, mastitis, latch issues, tongue tie issues, lactose allergies, colic, and reflux. Whew! It was an honor, *but* I am not ashamed to admit that for me, it also felt like a *tedious* chore.

I am so thankful for both my health nurse and my lactation consultant who helped me through this exhausting and beautiful chapter of life. If you are having issues or need support with breastfeeding, I encourage you to reach out to your local health nurse or, if you are in Canada, *La Leche League*.[1] Deciding how to nourish your tiny newborn is a responsibility all of us new moms have. If you formula feed—good for you! If you nurse—good for you! If you pump—good for you! No, really, I mean it—good for you. No matter how you feed your new baby, it is a lot of work. We deserve a pat on the back because it is true what they say—*fed is best*.

I had big dreams of feeding my children only organic and homemade baby food. What I had planned and envisioned was so different than my reality. I placed so much pressure on myself that I made early feeding with my first child harder than it needed to be. I accidentally turned early eating into a stressful time, when in hindsight, it should have been a happy and relaxing time. My children had allergies I was not aware of until they were older, which also made feeding them a tad more challenging.

As a veteran mother, now I have so much advice for the younger version of myself.

---

1   La Leche League Canada. (2019). Retrieved from https://www.lllc.ca/

- **Lean into Baby-led Weaning.**[2] This means allow your child to feed themselves, safely, right from the very start of weaning. Children love to explore different temperatures and textures. They have fun playing with the food, feeling included, and learning independence—and bonus, sometimes they actually manage to swallow some.

- **Choose a variety of safe and healthy foods** for your child. Allow them the freedom to try new foods without judgment or pressure. If they turn their nose up at a particular food, keep trying that food, casually, and perhaps after a few more relaxed tries, they might learn to enjoy it.

- **Practice with your children** while they learn to eat. Spend time with them, even when they are young; talk to them and make mealtime fun. It's never too early to start patterns and traditions.

- **Prepare for and *allow* the mess**; it is inevitable anyway.

- **Cherish this time together.** Take photos and videos. Embrace this chapter of life.

I found that the more my young children were given the opportunity to play, touch, and explore their food with their fingers, the more they ate. In time, all my children loved mealtime and exploring the different textures and tastes of food. By my third child, I had learned (from experience) that the less I stressed about forcing them to try a new food, the easier it was for them (and myself). I leaned into the messy, playful, and creative and focused on nurturing their curiosity while keeping them nour-

2   Rapley, G., & Murkett, T. (2019). *Baby-Led Weaning, Baby-Led Weaning: The Essential Guide to Introducing Solid Foods-and Helping Your Baby to Grow Up a Happy and Confident Eater,* New York: The Experiment.

ished and fed. I learned to just keep offering healthy foods in new ways, repeatedly.

Maybe your child is like mine and chooses to not eat something because of the texture. My middle child disliked mashed-up banana but loved eating a banana sliced up. To this day, my daughter will not eat a hard-boiled egg but loves eggs prepared every other way. My eldest is still not a fan of foods mixed together, but if you separate the food, he will eat it all, plus help himself to seconds. All my children love a variety of healthy and colorful foods and will consume more if I accept and acknowledge their idiosyncrasies, adjust the textures and presentation of the food, and encourage their curiosity and taste buds.

We also all have a happier experience if I sit down and eat with them, and this was true even at the toddler age.

I encourage you to unplug and reconnect with your littles, join them while they eat, and make mealtime a time they will remember and cherish, not a chore or stressful event.

If you feed your toddler all organic food—good for you! If you follow baby-led weaning—good for you! If you do not follow any meal plan for your toddler, that is okay, too! No matter what you feed your baby—good for you! Feeding toddlers is chaos on wheels; trust me, I get it. It is a lot of work. All of us moms who are feeding wriggly, curious, and noisy toddlers deserve a pat on the back.

Childhood Memories

When I was a young child, I remember excitedly making my school lunches. It was a staple in my house to have a PB&J (peanut butter and jam) sandwich in my lunchbox or as an after-school snack. I always had it on toast, to feel "fancy." Sometimes I still crave one. It's total comfort food for me. My dad used to enjoy peanut butter with sliced-up bananas on his sandwiches; this, too, became a childhood favorite of mine. Little did I know that the reason this was a staple in my house was because it was affordable and easy. PB&J was a common snack for many of us who grew up in the 80s or early 90s. However, it's become a "taboo" lunch staple for my children's generation—mostly due to children in the classroom who suffer from allergies, but also because children nowadays have little time to eat during the school day, and a sandwich takes too long to consume.

Making school lunches fun and nutritious while staying on a budget is a challenge for many of us moms. So, if you are in the chapter of life in which you're packing school lunches daily, you deserve a pat on the back.

As I write this, I have been a mother for 5,393 days. For the same amount of days, I have been responsible for what my children consume. This is both a beautiful responsibility and an absolute chore. My children are fourteen, twelve, and eleven years old. I sometimes feel like I live in my kitchen. If I am not preparing or cooking a meal, I am helping to clean up after one, putting away groceries, making a list, or preparing for school and work lunches. Between the three meals a day I offer and the one to three healthy snack options that are available to them throughout the day, it seems like my children are *always* eating. I often have to remind myself that my children's bodies and their hunger do not operate on the same "clock" as mine. We keep different hours, they are often going through growth spurts, and I have become adjusted to my personal routine and needs.

*I want my children to have a love and
appreciation for food as big as my love for
peanut butter.*

I want my children to grow up understanding, and appreciating the foods we consume. I think that is a wish most parents have for their children, but it often seems like a hard goal to accomplish. Children have inconsistent taste buds and can be picky eaters. Sometimes they will eat a certain food, sometimes they will not. I find it is vital to have a variety of options available to them, and I keep offering food again and again. I like to empower my children to make their own choices and decisions—with a little guidance, of course. Although it is quite hard for me to stop controlling what they eat, I have learned that by doing so, I guide them to make informed and healthy choices themselves. Now that I am raising and feeding "tweens" ("a youngster between ten and twelve years of age, considered too old to be a child and too young to be a teenager"[3]) and a teenager, I strive daily to educate them about the foods we eat and the benefits of each ingredient. I lead by example and use every opportunity to explain my choices.

If you control what your tween eats—good for you! If you allow them to make their own meals, some of which may be comprised of some unhealthy choices—good for you! No matter what you feed your tween and teen—good for you! Feeding young teenagers sometimes feels exhausting. They seem to be hungry all the time; not to mention, they can be moody and are navigating their way through the pangs of high school, social norms, and everything in between. They want to learn to be independent and make their own decisions, even if those decisions are unhealthy. All of us moms feeding tweens and teens deserve a pat on the back.

---

3   Tween. (2019). Dictionary.com. Retrieved from https://www.dictionary.com/browse/tween

Grilled Cheese Fail

My children and I love to cook and bake together. They found measuring and mixing the ingredients fun and interesting as young children, and we would always try a tiny nibble before the dish was ready. Memories of baking cookies with my mom flow through me every time I pull out the measuring cups with my own children.

I encourage and allow them to practice independence in the kitchen. All my kids can check the pantry, freezer, and fridge, make a grocery list, do a basic round of grocery shopping, meal prep, cook, bake, and help clean up. They have made countless mistakes in the kitchen, but each mistake is an opportunity to learn. One of my favorite memories is when one of them was learning to make a grilled cheese sandwich—but used a toaster rather than a frying pan or griddle. They were creative enough to put the toaster onto its side and try to slide the grilled cheese into it to cook. This ended with the smoke detector going off and a huge mess being made of the toaster. But it was a learning moment, and I could see the thought process behind it. We have also had the classics—the pancake-the-size-of-the-pan that was a disaster when we tried to flip it, the cookies that did not work out because of recipe creativity or measurement mistakes.

It is important for me to teach my children to cook. They can all prepare basic meals (with just a little help) such as French toast, eggs, cookies, pancakes, Hamburger Helper, chili, spaghetti, and soup. I love having them help me with more complex dinners too. They do not realize the lessons I am teaching them while they shuck the corn, peel the carrots, or help barbeque proteins.

We also love to garden and grow our own veggies and fruits. There is something so magical about planting a seed, tending to the plants, and then reaping its harvest. We try to grow tomatoes, snap peas, corn, peppers, lettuce, strawberries, raspberries, and onions as much as we can.

Trini To D'Bone

It is my goal to develop my children's taste buds, so that they grow up to be familiar with and to crave healthy and nutritious foods. We occasionally enjoy eating out and trying new restaurants and foods. Just recently, I tried doubles and goat curry from a local Trinidadian restaurant with some good friends of mine. I later took my children there with a friend who had grown up in Trinidad, and we spent the morning at the restaurant talking about Trinidadian culture and food and learning more about cardamom, cinnamon, cloves, habanero, cilantro, and pimento. I am so proud to say that not only did my kids try the food—two of them *loved* it. Watching them try bite after bite of this new food was exhilarating. I love my children's passion and curiosity for food and for life. They have also explored and enjoyed Brazilian, Italian, Thai, Mexican, Caribbean, and Asian dishes. Our favorites include arroz carreteiro, Bolognese, pad Thai, tacos, jerk chicken with peas and rice, and sushi. I love when we take our kids out to eat at our favorite eateries, but I especially love it when we try something new together. Together, we learn about the ingredients, textures, and tastes.

I AM learning to like tomatoes.

When I am with my children, I try very hard to never say, " I hate _____," but rather "I'm learning to like _____," when I dislike food. I am well aware that my little humans are constantly watching and learning from me, and I try very, very hard to set a good example as often as possible. A perfect example of this is my dislike of tomatoes. I *am* learning to like tomatoes; my daughter, on the other hand, *loves* cherry tomatoes. If I had stopped cooking with them or buying them just because I didn't like them, I would never have learned that she loves them.

My children had allergies I was not aware of until they were older, which also made feeding them a tad more challenging. Allergies provide another example of challenges with feeding children. My middle son cannot eat whole eggs, so sometimes we have had to adapt our meals accordingly. We have learned how to bake without eggs by using substitutes such as (but not limited to) coconut milk, cornstarch, peanut butter, and applesauce. By being adaptable, we have learned to make some yummy, delicious, and wholesome eggless meals and desserts.

As we enter the teenage years, I realize it is time to empower my children to decide for themselves, to cook for themselves, and to learn the consequences involved in both. The meals do not have to be grand, but practicing the basics is a very important lesson in cooking and in life. Honing knife skills and safety, practicing cooking eggs, learning how to properly wash dishes, learning to multitask and act on impulse, and learning, as James Howell said, *"not to cry over spilled milk."*[4] Your children, like yourself, will make many mistakes in the kitchen and in their food choices. Getting the fundamentals right is imperative, and so is *not* giving up.

Many parents who are expecting their bundle(s) of joy are full of optimism and enthusiasm when talking about, planning, and imagining the joys of feeding and raising healthy children, only to realize that the day-to-day grind and reality of nourishing your child can sometimes be more difficult and exhausting than hoped.

---

4   "Crying Over Spilled Milk." (2009). The Grammarphobia blog. Retrieved from https://www.grammarphobia.com/blog/2009/09/crying-over-spilled-milk.html

My most honest advice is to schedule time each day to plan what you and your family will consume; have easy-to-grab, healthy options ready and available; and surround yourself as much as possible with supportive friends, family, or community members while learning to feed your child. And most of all, always listen to your gut instinct and your baby.

Remember, you know your baby best!

Much Love,
Charleyne
#coachcharleybrown

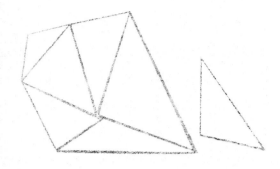

BEING MAMA

*Communicating with a toddler
is difficult.
It's trying to explain what color
the number 4 smells like . . .*

-Author Unknown

Chapter Three

Embracing My Journey

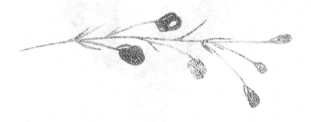

"I'll spend half of my life in the state of menopause; I had to own it and love it!"

Liz Vardan

ig: @the__m__word

Liz Vardan

Born in Istanbul, with strong Mediterranean genes, (Ozlem) Liz moved to Toronto with her family at seventeen year old. Funny how life is—she met her husband back in Istanbul ten years later. Her years as a psychology student, combined with her yoga practice over the past couple decades, served as a great base. Goddess boot camp in Kripalu was the first place she came to know of her powers: the power of intention, visualization, and meditation. Liz now uses her powers to pave the way and break the taboos surrounding menopause. Every single woman reading this anywhere in the world will either go through menopause or has gone through it already. No exception. Not a single woman will be spared. What Liz didn't know was that she'd go through it in her late thirties. This may seem unfortunate to some, but Liz took it as a sign that she must help, guide, and support women all over the world to understand their body - mind connection. As mother to a daughter, Liz feels a great responsibility to share her experience and help women manifest their goals and dreams and deal with hormones naturally. Now as a successful real estate broker, an entrepreneur, a yoga teacher, and a mother of a tween-to-be, Liz keeps her sight on her *why*—her daughter Mira.

"She remembered who she was, and the game changed." -Lalah Deliah

This is my journey of coming back to myself and discovering new ways of living and being me.

One day, I woke up in fear. Fear of not being able to get up. I could barely move my legs. They were sore and shaking. It felt like I was about to come down with the flu, that type of awkward joint pain. But the pain kept coming back every morning, with no flu. Same went for the feverish feeling. I could feel my body tingle and boil from the inside; the feeling would reach the top of my head and burn. This sensation was new to me but it became very familiar over time. This is when the anxiety found its way in, I think.

I remember one day having to lie down and calm my breath by counting. One of my first panic attacks ever, just because my friend was a few minutes late dropping off my daughter. *This had happened before, so why did it feel like my heart was coming out of my chest now and why was I crying? What was this I was experiencing?* My mind was playing tricks on me, making the situation seem worse, scenario after scenario.

I had never felt this way before. Anxiety is a scary beast. It held me back from living my life fully. And the mood swings were the big, bold cherry on top. I would snap, get angry easily, then feel guilty and burst into tears. It was like being pregnant and PMSing all at the same time. As a mother, this was the biggest challenge I have ever experienced. And it affected all my relationships greatly. How do you mother when all your emotions are all over the place . . . I was functioning on fumes alone and feeling not enough for my daughter.

This went on for a couple years until, only a few days after my thirty-ninth birthday I found out I was experiencing menopause. All my hormone levels were at post-menopause! I sat in the doctor's office, confused and scared, as my doctor passed me a note on which she had scribbled down a website address. That was it—read up and learn. Yes, I was grateful that all my symptoms only meant menopause, but I was also shocked and filled with even more anxiety. I cried all the way home, not because menopause is sad but because this is how I coped with all my wacky hormones, or lack thereof. Everything changed that day.

My husband had made a comment a few weeks before about my wild hair, joking that he didn't know if my wild hair was making me crazy or if my craziness was making my hair shoot straight up into the air. I knew the two had to be connected. And there it was.

The dizzy spells came out of nowhere, making me feel like the entire world was swinging. The first time I had experienced this, it was extremely scary, and I knew it had to be a sign of something. Little did I know this would happen again and again and again. When you think of the physical symptoms of menopause, dizzy spells don't usually come to mind. But there I was in the kitchen, feeling like the earth was moving under me. The second time it happened was six months later. Then, weekly.

Electrical shocks under my skin, randomly all over my body, pinching me. It was like some sort of a torture method, made worse by the millions of assumptions swirling in my head, the unknown as to why this might be happening. If you ask me, this must be the literal meaning of your nerves being shot. One nerve at a time burning up as my anxiety levels continued to increase.

The tight feeling around my throat felt like someone was choking me. I felt like I was possessed, although some days were better than others. When I had the courage to get it checked out, all the tests came back negative, yet again. It was anxiety finding a way to express itself.

Memory loss and brain fog took me by surprise. If you asked anyone around me, they might have agreed that I was losing my mind. I had to put triple the effort into everything just to keep up. I used little sticky notes, but even then, I would forget whatever it was before I had a chance to put it down on paper. This memory loss seemed to get worse over time. All over again, I had pregnancy brain. These mental symptoms were sometimes more difficult to deal with than the physical symptoms. I was so used to being in control, sharply focused, taking care of millions of things at once, like most moms. Now I could barely concentrate on my work and my family life simultaneously. It was like watching my life melt in front of my eyes. I was so exhausted physically, but I couldn't lift a finger to do anything about it.

These intense moments of fear were unfamiliar to a once strong and confident woman. It felt like something had taken over my body and emotions; nothing of me belonged to me anymore. It shapeshifted and changed every day. For a person who had never experienced fear and anxiety, it was like being dropped off the edge of a cliff, not knowing what hit you on the way down. It crept into my life without warning. At thirty-nine years old, early menopause was a big shock. The fact that I now know what was causing all the headaches, dizziness, joint pain, and many other symptoms was a huge relief and a blessing. Yet in those moments when the symptoms hit, I still felt completely lost. It was chaotic. The physical symptoms were causing more and more anxiety, keeping me in my head. I couldn't recognize myself. I was in a downward spiral, losing control of my body and mind.

I had always been a strong mama: strong-willed with strong emotions and a strong body. Now all the strength in my life got replaced with fragility, sensitivity, and weakness. But I was not going to let this take its toll on me. I grieved over the person I used to be and knew now it was time to snap out of it. I needed to rebirth myself, rebuild, and become a newer and better version of myself. I needed to make the decision to embrace this new challenge!

I will spend more than half of my life in the state of menopause, so I had to own it and love it—love me. Even though early menopause may sound like early aging, I can take it as an opportunity to tackle aging when it is easier to preserve my body. I knew instinctively that I did not want to reject this new physical body or try to reverse the process. Well, my mind wanted to reject it, but I had to get out of my head and bring it down to my heart. I had to accept it from the bottom of my heart. But no matter how much you accept yourself nothing prepares you for the lack of support from your partner. In my case not being heard or understood made everyday a challenge as we grew further apart.

I have always believed that the solutions to our mental, physical, and emotional challenges are hidden within us. I never doubted this. Even though I wanted to tackle my menopause in an *au natural* way, I had to get information about hormone replacement therapy, to eliminate it in a way. My appointment with a hormone specialist finally came seven months after I asked for a referral; I realize that might sound outrageous, but I assure you it's quite normal in the Canadian healthcare system. The day had arrived; a doctor would explain the pros and cons and maybe check me and advise me. Excited to ask questions, I walked into her office, and five minutes later came out completely crushed. I was told it shouldn't even be an option not to take hormones and that if I thought otherwise, I was wasting her time. She also told me to freeze my daughter's eggs when she reached the age of eighteen. She printed off some general information and told me to read it and come back only if I was willing to take hormone replacement therapy (HRT).

I took this experience as a sign, a great example of creating your reality. I believe I brought this experience because I already knew I did not want to take hormones. It might have been an easy and simple solution in the short term, but I want to experience my body and emotions just the way they are. For me, HRT would be like covering up the reality. I am responsible for my own life and through my choices, I co-create my own reality! This is the mentality driving how I live now. Manifesting my life, one day at a time.

I acknowledge. I accept. I embrace. I love myself!

Just the way I am.

I am enough.

Since then, I have been using Emotional Freedom Technique (EFT), combined with my affirmations. The quality of my life has increased greatly. Tapping utilizes the body's energy meridian points, a compelling ability for healing. My fears dissipated one at a time, and my symptoms eased as I took my power back.

There is an ancient Zen story of a man who was walking at night; he fell off the rock above a valley in the pitch black. Knowing how deep the valley was, he hung off a branch, shivering in fear. He hung until dawn, thinking he could die at any second if his hands slipped. With the daylight, he discovered he was only a few inches off another big rock where he could have rested comfortably.

From my own experience, I can say that fear is only a few inches deep, no more. As I tell my daughter—fear is fake. You might have heard the acronym F.E.A.R: False Evidence Appearing Real. Fear is a distraction and will only take away from the present moment. Once you embrace that thought, so much more space opens up in your life.

With yoga and meditation already deeply rooted in my life, I feel like I have had an advantage on my journey to my new self. My holistic approach fit seamlessly into my life, creating space physically and emotionally. I have become more spiritual and more creative with my yoga practice. Some days, it is more vigorous and other days, more meditative. In the beginning, accepting each day as a different experience was a challenge. But I embrace the challenge. Be it dancing or running, whatever it might be for you, I strongly believe moving your body and doing what you love will help heal your body. Once the body is happy, so is the mind.

Another way to keep physically healthy is to have sex regularly. It is great exercise and a great way to connect with your partner. Vaginal dryness and pain are also symptoms of menopause, but they are not talked about as much as the others. It is now time to break the taboos. The more sex you have, the less discomfort you're in. There are many other benefits to having sex, such as heart health, a healthy immune system, and of course, a better mood. Own your body and don't shy away from it. This is what kept my relationship from completely falling apart.

I am grateful day and night for every incredible moment in my life, for my daughter, and for my experiences. With early menopause, even though it seemed like my life crumbled one day at a time, now I see how much better life actually is. I am healthier. I value myself more. I take care of myself better.

I describe menopause as an awakening, a woman becoming. A wise woman! No more playing small, no more thinking small. I allow the wisdom to flow through me and guide me as I embrace my life as it is now.

Walking the early menopause road with confidence, I now let my hair down and let it be wild. It is more beautiful than ever before.

> *"Be fearless in the pursuit of what sets your soul on fire."* -Unknown

Driven Mama

Section 2

Featuring:
Shannon-Lee Figsby
Habbiba Jessica Zaman
Jenna Knight
Valerie Steele
Erica Lambert

Dreamer
Restless
Inspired
Vivacious
Entrepreneur
Nonstop

Being a driven mama means you are a woman who is determined, motivated, and energized! You will find that the women in these chapters have juggled relationships, life, career, and motherhood. Some were bosswoman entrepreneurs before being a mama and had to learn how to rock a stroller in their day-to-day. Others found their passion after child birth. Some women found their strength to grow in motherhood and made fundamental choices for the future of their family. Some never knew they would be a mama, some always knew they would.

Being driven is about being bound and determined to do your absolute best and learning when to embrace the support of your community. Being driven also means you need to find a balance in your new chaotic world. You will manage twenty things at once, but you will learn to prioritize what needs to be done, for the sake of your kids and your sanity! (Trust me, the laundry can wait!) There is a lot of change that comes with motherhood and you may be too stubborn to accept that you can't do it all by yourself. Sometimes you need a little help, and that is OK!

Don't let anyone else write your guide to parenting, do what feels right to YOU. Your intuition will be your guide. This may mean enrolling your child in daycare, so you can do your nine-to-five or your school work. You may have to work late nights, or you may have your child in tow to your new business . . . whatever your struggle may be, just breathe. You can do it!

Mama, accept those snuggles while they are still abundant, then power through that paperwork; because this overflowing cup of love is temporary.

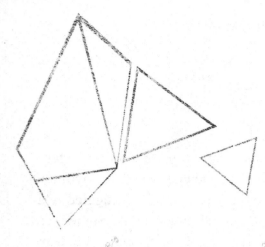

BEING MAMA

Some days I'm killing it as Mom. Other days, I call my kid the dog's name, burn dinner, forget it's garbage day, rewash the same load of laundry three times, and remember yesterday's doctor's appointment just as I'm finally falling asleep.

@momtransparenting

Chapter Four

The Business of Mom-Bossing

"Some women suffer from postpartum depression. Not me. I had postpartum awakening."

Shannon-Lee Figsby

www.academiededanseelite.com | www.studio-couture.com

ig: @academiededanseelite | @fitmamashannon
@shannydancer | @wearestudiocouture
fb: @academiededanseelite | @fitmamashannon
@wearestudiocouture | @shannon.figsby

Shannon-Lee Figsby

Shannon-Lee Figsby knew from a very young age that she wanted to spend her life creating. Her formal education came in the form of a bachelor's degree with a double-major in journalism and communications from Concordia University, while also spending nearly twenty years training for a career in professional dance.

Shannon is now the proud owner and director of the internationally recognized dance studio Academie de danse Elite Inc., in Ile Perrot, QC., home to the 2017 World Dance Champions. Shannon worked as a professional dancer for many years, appearing in many Montreal stage shows, commercials, and music videos. She is also a former professional CFL Cheerleader for the Montreal Alouettes.

After having her first child at the age of twenty-nine, and enduring an intense struggle to lose the seventy pounds she gained while pregnant with him, Shannon was compelled to start a second company called Fit Mama Shannon, which centered around health and wellness with a specific focus on helping women, particularly mothers, become their best selves. While she still adored working with and teaching youngsters, after becoming a mother herself, she knew she had a gift she could offer women who may be struggling like she was as well.

Shannon now owns a third company called Studio Couture, a dance and fitness-wear company. Shannon is an Amazon top one hundred best selling author of, *I'm 30, Now What?!* She lives in a suburb of Montreal, QC, with her husband Chris, and her two-year-old son, Dublin.

"I am not lucky. You know what I am? I am smart. I am talented. I take advantage of the opportunities that come my way and I work really, really hard. Don't call me lucky. Call me a badass." -Shonda Rhimes

 am positioned in front of a class of twenty-one teenage girls aged thirteen to seventeen. I am trying desperately to lead a warm-up that includes ten minutes of dance cardio, followed by ten minutes of conditioning, stretching, and abdominal work, before we get into another forty minutes of dance instruction. I have done this same warm-up, changing nothing but the songs, for the past seven years. But today, I am certain, I will die. I will not get through this warm-up alive.

Today, you see, I neglected to realize that actually, I have changed something other than the music. Today, as opposed to last time I gave a full-out dance class nearly one year ago, everything has changed. Today, I am wearing three sports bras, and despite the triple bagging of my thirty-six triple Ds, my girls are aching with every kick-ball-change. Today, I am so exhausted that the simple act of breathing in air hurts my windpipe. Today, I am fifty pounds heavier than I was a year ago and I almost can't stand looking at myself in the mirror. Today, I have a new student—my four-week-old baby boy, who's watching me instruct the class from his bucket seat in the corner of the studio.

Today, I am not just a dance studio owner teaching a dance class.

Today, I am also a mom. The problem is, everyone—including myself—seems to have forgotten that the last little differentiating factor is actually the biggest game changer that's ever existed.

That day, two and a half years ago, was a defining moment for me. Since we've been talking about the past, let me give you a little background. For my entire life, the only thing I've ever wanted to do is dance. Perform, teach, own my own studio—I wanted it all. I started dancing at the age of three and never really stopped, competing until the end of high school, and teaching and performing throughout university and the years that followed. When an opportunity arose to open my own dance school with a (now former) business partner eight years ago, I jumped all over it. All my dreams were coming true.

I poured my heart and soul, my blood, sweat, and tears, all my free time and energy, and sometimes my own money, into Academie de danse Elite. It was my baby, and I was willing to do anything to see it flourish, and my students along with it. After I got engaged in 2013, people would ask me when I wanted to have kids. I would say I already have 250 of them. My students were like my surrogate children, and we were a family in our own right. Until I gave birth to my own child in November of 2015, and I realized that shit was about to get real.

I was determined not to let my status as a new mother affect my ability to run a growing company. I wanted to prove to everyone that I could do it all—be a wife, mother, and a badass business woman—and oh, guess what, I wasn't even going to put my kid in daycare. I could do it all. I would be a supermom. Who needs sleep? What I didn't realize, however, was that by not accepting the significant and inevitable changes, which come about as a result of bringing a baby into the mix, I was doing myself a huge disservice. I mean, no one should be teaching a dance class when they're still bleeding from their hoo-ha.

My son's first year on this earth was also the most challenging year for my studio, and brought about many changes that no one could have seen coming. And for this, I thank him. As I mentioned in my previous book that I co-authored, some women suffer from postpartum depression after giving birth. Not me. I had postpartum awakening.

There were so many moments where I wished I had someone to turn to—besides my amazing family, friends, and clients who became friends—for advice on how to balance this whole baby and business deal. So that's why I decided to write this chapter. Here, I'd like to share with you the top five things related to mom-ing and mom-bossing that I wished someone would have shared with me before having my son:

Your vision for the future of your business will become extremely clear. Go with it. For some, this may mean realizing the business world isn't for them. For me, this meant the total opposite. I dove in head first making changes in every single area of my studio that I thought would benefit my students—including buying out my business partner.

It's funny to think about it now, but before I had my son, I looked at other people's kids just like that—other people's kids. Becoming a mother added what I felt like was a new layer of responsibility to my job. I suddenly became vehemently passionate about not only the dance training my students were receiving, but also the life lessons I suddenly felt so graciously responsible to impart upon them. The fact that their parents were trusting me with this was no small thing.

I shifted the focus of the competitive program within my studio to mental preparation and coached my dancers, more psychologically than physically. There were small additions; like "Pride Night" before big competitions, where the girls dedicated their performance on stage the following day to someone who mattered deeply to them in their lives; to smaller ones such as distributing "Power Pak's" before competing with silly, but fun items like Ring Pops, bouncy balls, and other pun-allowing knick knacks.

I added a leadership program to the studio and shifted the focus of the teaching assistant program to one that wasn't just about getting free help, but also about giving our teaching assistants the tools necessary to become amazing teachers.

Looking at it now, I guess I started coaching my dancers exactly as I would want my son coached. Letting them know that no matter what, they were loved. Coming off stage after a less than stellar performance was no longer a "good try," but "good job."

My approach worked. My first year owning the studio alone, we became the 2017 World Dance Champions, by far the biggest accomplishment of my career to date. And you know what? The person I was before having my son would not have that banner hanging in her studio. But that's okay. Because she didn't have the same priorities that I do. Because we were not the same person anymore.

Your priorities will change—and that's okay. Before I had my son, I had absolutely no qualms about working sixteen-hour days and getting home from the studio at midnight. If there was work to be done, who cared if we ate dinner at midnight? My two equally top priorities were my clients, and ensuring my business was running as smoothly and efficiently as possible. Now, while the business is just as important, so is the business of bath time and bedtime stories. The fact is, as much as you might want to tell yourself that you're the same person you were before having a baby, you aren't. You, quite simply, are not. And that's not a bad thing. You've brought a new life into this world, and that new life is bringing some new perspective to yours. Personally this hit me hard. It particularly hit me hard in the body image department. As a dancer, your livelihood is directly impacted by your appearance. It's just a reality of the industry. If you have a tendency towards the extreme, as I do, this reality can lead to an unhealthy obsession with being thin, and in my case, an eating disorder that lasted nearly a decade.

However, as I mentioned in my previous book, *I'm 30, Now What?!*—when you become pregnant as a recovering anorexic, you do not restrict yourself. No matter what you think you need, becoming a mama is about what the baby needs. And for me, that started in the womb.

So I ate for nine months. I mean, gawd did I eat! Everything and anything I wanted or had denied myself for the better portion of my adolescent and adult life. Seventy pounds later, I gave birth to a beautiful, healthy, and very average-sized seven pounds, two-ounce baby boy. The rest was all me! But after having Dublin, for the first time in my life, I wasn't in a massive rush to lose the weight. Unlike many women (whom I'm not judging—you do you!) who start exercising at the six-week postpartum mark once their doctor has given them the green light, I preferred the six-month mark, hence the near-death experience teaching a bunch of teenagers I described earlier.

Whereas the pre-baby me was hiking three days after major knee surgery to avoid "sluggishness," a.k.a. weight gain, the post-baby Shannon simply had other priorities. One major priority was being able to produce enough breast milk to continue nursing my son as long as I wanted, so calorie restriction wasn't an option. And for those first few months, I'd choose sleep over working out. (In. A. Freaking. Heartbeat.) Dublin was born in November, 2015, and I lost the first ten pounds in May, 2016. While the baby weight is now gone completely, the healthy habits are here to stay. Not just for myself, but as an example for my son and future children, of a mom who prioritizes health over all else, regardless of the circumstances.

You actually, really, cannot do it all. Get some help. Figure out two things about your business right away—what you LOVE doing, and what can ONLY be done by you. Delegate the rest. Hire office staff. Hire a cleaning person. Heck, do the same for your house if you can afford it (I couldn't at first). Do the same with a meal service. Do what you have to do so you can spend your time on things you love to do, such as running your business and being with your family. If you're anything like me, the word "delegate" makes you shudder. Embrace the shivers, Mama. (I know.) I KNOW you think that you are the only person who can draft a reminder email perfectly, choose and order the most exquisite costume, and ensure it's expertly sized on 456 children, AND keep desk accessories in your office exactly how they should be, and you might be right. But you know what's better than perfect?

Done.

Not just done, but done and home, with my son and husband, enjoying their company instead of stressing over what looms unfinished at the studio.

Although delegating was difficult for me, it was made easier after identifying what it was about my business that I was truly passionate about—what filled my cup. For me, it was always the interaction I had with the students and their parents. So communication became my focus, and my main one at that. Everything, and I mean everything, that wasn't completely student-centric or had a direct impact on the interpersonal relationships with the people I surrounded myself with every day became the responsibility of someone else. Teachers were asked to choose their own costumes and complete size measurements for their students, and then submit their data to me. I hired an accounting firm that did everything via that famous cloud somewhere out there in cyberspace. I mean, all I had to do was snap a picture of a receipt or invoice with my phone and "POOF"—look Ma, accounting's done! I hired a law firm I only needed to meet with one time a year to keep the minute book of my corporation up to date, legally. For every responsibility, I had a "guy" (or girl!) who could do it for me, so I could focus on what I really loved doing. Besides, nobody is good at everything anyways, and if they claim to be, they're too good to be true.

Be real—other moms will love you more for it. In the early days of having my son, I was so afraid that my clients would perceive becoming a mother as a weakness since I was the "get it done" partner in the studio. This was probably the same mentality that led me to believe I had to resume teaching classes four weeks postpartum. (How wrong I was.) Who are my clients? Kids. What do kids have? Moms. Moms who have been there, moms who see the struggle, and moms who see through the bullshit if you claim there are no struggles. These are your people.

I found my people in the place I knew best—my own studio. The sisterhood of mothers is one that I quickly found transcends age, language, socio-economic status, and even client-service provider relationships.

I vividly remember the day I walked out of the studio and into the hallway smack dab in the middle of a class I was teaching. My period was back for the first time since having my child, and it was back with a vengeance. Seeing the horror on my face, one mom in her mid-fifties asked what was wrong.

"The super-sized tampon I was wearing just fell straight out of my vagina," I told her, completely serious. "Is this normal during your first postpartum period?"

She assured me it was, and that I could expect many other fun surprises I hadn't yet been warned about, like having this period lasts weeks on end (and it did), or peeing every time I laughed (I don't yet—but give me time, I only have one kid!).

The thing is, she didn't even bat an eye. This was the same mom who I had always been somewhat intimidated by—a police officer with a straightforward attitude and strong opinions she frequently made known. Because she had been there, and like me, she was not afraid to be real about it. Because she was my people. My son found a surrogate family within the walls of my studio, quite literally. And in turn, I found my mom-tribe. I nearly lost my shit one afternoon when my son was about eleven months old and starting his first bout of gastroenteritis. I was feeding him, when all of a sudden he stood up on my thighs, looked me in the eyes, and projectile vomited straight into my face. And then did it again. I was covered in vomit, quite literally from head to waist, concerned for my son while at the same time on the verge of tears, considering I felt as if my dignity as a studio owner was hanging by a thread. I should mention this was about three weeks after my former business partner and I split, and I had purchased the studio! But before I could lose it completely, a studio-mom swooped in, took my son, and stripped him while passing him off to another mom. As she sent her daughter to get me some clothes from the merchandise table, she wiped the vomit from my face and hair, while instructing her son to start scrubbing the carpets. She sent me home swiftly, and when I came in the next day, there was no evidence of anything that had happened the night before. While this particular mom and her entire family have become dear, dear friends of mine, it was crystal clear to me in that moment, I was surrounded by love.

Be real Mama, and the authenticity will come back to you in spades. You will figure out what works for you. If you are anything like me, you were winging your child's first year of life. Maybe you still are. The fact that my studio was open at night posed a particular set of issues for our little family considering the fact that I was still nursing. A "normal" sleep schedule wasn't possible, and so many other factors.

However, eventually, we got into a groove and figured out what worked for us. My son came to work with me every single day and still does, until Dad, Grammy, or Nanny picks him up for dinner and bedtime a few nights a week. He is surrounded by other kids and I'll never have to look for a babysitter as long as I live. And he gets to see first-hand that it's not just the dads who get to be CEOs . . . his mama isn't doing so bad herself!

And neither are you. After all, this is what "being Mama" is all about!

Chapter Five

I Am . . .

*"I would not allow anyone else to continue
writing my narrative for me."*

Habiba Jessica Zaman

www.HABIBAZAMAN.com

ig: @habibti_zaman
fb: @habibajessicazaman | @northstarofgeorgia

Habiba Jessica Zaman

Habiba Jessica Zaman-Tran, NCC LPC, has a master's degree in professional counseling specializing in trauma, and is the therapist and owner of North Star of Georgia Counseling. With fifteen years of work experience in the counseling field including counseling, advocacy, guidance, and education, she believes that as awareness of one's fears, perception, desires, and strengths increase, one can make successful life changes. Self-awareness by becoming more honest with oneself, can initiate the authenticity that often results in healing, transformation, and living a fuller life. She has thirteen publications that started with a children's book titled, *But I'm Just Playing* published in 2012, followed by *Beautifully Bare, Undeniably You*, award-winning *Dear Time, Are You on My Side?*, Amazon best-seller *Dear Love, I'm Ready for You*, and *You've Got This, Mama* released in 2018. Habiba is of Bangladeshi and American descent. She has two children and lives in Atlanta, Georgia with her family.

Being Mama . . . what a powerful image. We embody the strength of will to focus and excel in our careers while maintaining the nurturing, guidance and softness of our greatest role, Mama. We have the best of both worlds in being able to follow our intellectual passions as well as be present for the recitals and skinned knees. We thrive in the work force and have the responsibility of being the greatest influencers in these babies lives. Here is the truth. Looking from the outside, I seem like a put together, well-adjusted power house that is slaying the world of therapy, entrepreneurship, authorhood, the role of caregiver, interior designer of all things festive, judge and jury of brotherly injustice and priestess of the moon, keeping watch and surrounding my boys in an aura of protection and love. You may see Facebook and Instagram posts of an active single mama kicking ass when it comes to playing with the kids and teaching them about the world, alongside the posts of spreading inspiration as a therapist, business owner and writer. It seems like I've got it all, and I am managing it all with the grace of Audrey Hepburn with wing tipped eyeliner and stilettos. Even as I write these words, I feel the quickening of my pulse at the base of my throat. I feel the heaviness in my chest and the tears that are threatening my composure as a warning from my psyche that I am about to reveal something not many have the privilege to witness. Embodying Mama desensitizes you to vulnerabilities of what it means to be human at times and habituates the need to temper down the emotional side of ourselves. Having too many roles to play has become my norm and a part of my identity is being able to manage all of this beautifully. I no longer have a plate that's full, no my loves, I have a platter and it is rapidly overflowing. In maintaining this façade of boss mama, a part of my identity threatens to be lost in the glitz of the constant chaos, the part that I am not a machine, but rather a beautiful soul with a beating and most often, bleeding heart.

Let me start by saying that I would not have it any other way. People ask far too often if it isn't just too difficult to manage without a partner. Parents everywhere would be able to empathize with the daily struggles of managing life with children and yes, it is challenging at times, though not as difficult as it was with a partner who was not a partner in parenting. These days, yes, the responsibility falls on me to get them up, ready, fed, dropped off at school on time, then picked up from school, homework, studying, play time, dinner and finally our night time rituals of bath, daily affirmations, gratitude for each other and back to bed. This list does not include the executive details of running a private practice, seeing trauma clients back-to-back, supporting my therapists who look to me for guidance, and then the maintenance of the house with cleaning, groceries, small repairs, and the absolute heinous act of doing laundry. You see what I mean by an overflowing platter? And yet, I would not have it any other way. If it needs to get done, I do it, and if I cannot manage it this time, I cope with the reality of having limits and it goes onto the next set of to do lists. I no longer have to beg and nag and ask and drag someone to help me, to please just do something. There is a tremendous sensation of freedom and independence that comes from that.

The kids and I have a flow and aside from the normal hiccups of tantrums, hurt feelings or forgotten bookbags, they know what I expect of them, and there is a simplicity of existence that did not exist before. I'm sounding incredibly confident in my competency and self-reliance don't you think? The journey to find this assurance has been a long, winding, treacherous, tearful, and at times, a path filled with gut-wrenching fear and self-doubt.

The narrative of my marriage is no different than those who have experienced a failed relationship where two people were just not compatible with one another. He was who he was, I am who I am, and our values just did not match up. We are two extremes in personality and there is no way to find a middle ground. My standards will always be too high and as much as I would try to compromise, it will not be enough for me, and it would be giving everything from his side. It is just that simple. It is the acceptance of that simplistic definition that helped me to go ahead with the divorce. Before that, I was trapped in the quicksand of confusion, betrayal, and despair of how and why my life had turned out the way it had. I couldn't comprehend what I had done wrong for him to have turned away from me, to take his love away. I tolerated disrespect and exclusion from his family, I handed him freedom to explore his hobbies and friendships while I gave up mine, I took on the brunt of childrearing and maintaining the home, I worked only as much to make sure I was home for him and the children, I allowed my body to give into his desires even when I would tear. His comment of "you'll get wet eventually, you always do," when I was physically unresponsive because I did not feel sexually aroused, chipped away at my ability to stand my ground and set any boundaries. There was late-night messaging that would take place in the bathroom, or late-night phone calls that came through, that I turned away from because I did not have access to the phone records. I was given a specific amount for each month to handle all the household expenses because I was not allowed to access his bank accounts, and he would not create a new one with me even though he had a joint account with his mother. Each day was just like any other day, until one day I looked back and I couldn't recognize myself anymore. My friends had begun to share their concerns that the light that once shone so brightly, was barely an ember. When I would present these concerns, I would be met with comments such as being too sensitive, making a big deal out of nothing, and being too proud. I was too much for him. I had too much fire and anger, and I was too cold and calculated. At the same time, I wasn't caring enough, not loving enough, and not understanding enough. If I had taken on a new client that was more than "the ten to fifteen hours a week," I would be met with comments about putting my career above the needs of my children, and how he thought I was never supposed to neglect the children in that manner. In an attempt to tone down parts of my personality, I began to lose myself completely. I had become what my father called, "a shell without a soul." I refused to see the extent of damage to my self-esteem and worth, and as a result of this form of internalizations, I began to fall ill. My body began to shut down every four months, where I would end up in the hospital. I would have coughs that wouldn't ease, hives that manifested out of thin air, and all sorts of ailments that could not be medically explained—for I was a relatively healthy young woman.

My goal was to make it work for the children. It wasn't that bad, he took care of the family, most of the finances, and he was a great playmate for the children. We began to go to marriage counseling where more things unraveled. He shared that he didn't necessarily want to marry me (a comment he would make often during arguments), but he wanted to make sure no one else did. He shared that if I would become financially stable or successful, that he feared I would leave him because he loved me so much. He sobbed to the therapist saying, "if I saw myself the way other people did, that I would realize that I could have more and leave him, and he understands that all of this was wrong, but it's all because he was so afraid to lose me." Thankfully, by this time I was a practicing mental health therapist, and I was able to see through these behaviors and call them out for what they were, emotional and mental abuse. These actions worked on the twenty-three-year-old that loved and married him a decade before, but it wouldn't work for who I was at this point. What held me there for another year was my children. I was burdened with the heavy responsibility of maintaining stability of their home, and not exposing them to the hurt and instability of a broken home. I was intimately aware of the damage that can do to a child, I was once that child. So I stayed. When I caught him sneaking out of the house at 3:00 a.m. and not coming back until 7:00 a.m., I stayed. Even though it continued after I had confronted him because his explanation was he would walk around Walmart or go on long drives contemplating why his wife didn't love him anymore.

When we would discipline our eldest son based on an agreement we came to as a unit, I would hear him telling my son that he understands, and that mommy is just being angry and mean . . . I stayed. Until the day our marriage therapist called me out, asking how I would feel if my sons would be sitting in front of her in thirty years because they do not know how to have healthy relationships because they would repeat the dysfunctional one they saw growing up—that was the day where my perspective began to shift. I began to see how much more damage would come by attempting to super-glue this rapidly crumbling marriage, and how it would affect the lives and futures of my children. Then finally, the truth that I so vehemently tried to push aside would aggressively make itself known. I was driving to the office and having another venting session with my dearest childhood friend, when she asked me, "what would be the point of all of this *Jesu*, that you have sacrificed yourself for your kids and at the end of the day losing them anyways because of how he is painting you to them?" I felt slapped by her words. I began trembling until I lost all control over my composure and completely unraveled. All of this was for them, and all my kids would see is this monster that I had become. I was the mean, loud, angry, rigid mother, while he was the playful, quiet, victim of a father. They would see mommy ok, and then completely explode. What they wouldn't hear is that he would say critical and insulting things, often challenging my stance on how his family would treat me or why I believed, based on my training, the kids should not be exposed to PG-13 movies or teen video games at the age of five and three, with comments like, "is it just your pride? Are you trying to pick a fight?" This would then escalate with further jabs. Then I would get up to cool down because my husband is not standing up for me or my children, or understanding logical age guidelines, but he would follow me around the house from room to room, until he cornered me and I would react because I was triggered. The children wouldn't see any of that, all they perceived was one moment everything was ok, and the next, mommy is losing her shit and poor daddy is being yelled at for no reason. What is the point of accepting all of this hatred and abuse if I am to lose my kids in the process? Enough was enough. I went through the process of filing for divorce in spite of his threats and lack of support from my family. Being strong was my only option. These two amazing little humans were my sole reason for each ragged breath I was taking, and I would be damned if I lost them because of anything short of something that only I had done. I would not allow anyone else to continue writing my narrative for me.

I won't pretend to tell you that the path was easy or that I valiantly triumphed through the hardship. I saw a side of him that I could not have imagined. The viciousness, vindictiveness, and pure hatred that spewed off of him because I had taken away his perfect image. He followed through with his threats, and if it wasn't for my strong group of friends to hold me together when the shadow nearly engulfed me, I would not have made it through. This process also brought to my awareness that I no longer knew who I was or who I had once been. I was a shell without a soul . . . one night after the kids had been tucked safely in bed, I sat down with a pen in hand to slowly, gently try to reintroduce and reveal myself . . . to me. That night was where the "I am" activity was created.

I would like you to work through this therapeutic activity with me. Take stock of the ways that you have grown, changed, and the progress made thus far, in who you are and who you have become. Although it may at first feel self-congratulatory, you should celebrate all growth in the right direction and be proud of your newfound motivation and enhanced self-insight. Be explicit in identifying the transformation and avoid the common trap of taking these things for granted. They are not inevitable; it is absolutely possible to grow older but not wiser. However, you worked hard to get where you are, and in doing so, you are embracing your potential to live your best life. Whereas you may have lived hours, days, or decades without self-awareness, you likely have now arrived (or will soon arrive) at a place where you can recognize and articulate the magnificence of who you are.

When you are ready, challenge yourself to complete the statement "I am . . ." This should be more than just a sentence— although that is a tremendous beginning. Dig deep and be as abstract as you need to be. Think of what makes you uniquely, undeniably you. Think of how you see yourself existing and moving through this world. Again, recognize that even after all of the growth you have accomplished, this process can be hard. Do not be discouraged. When you have spent a lifetime—or even fragments of a lifetime—being made to believe that you are inadequate or unworthy, it is difficult to imagine yourself as anything more. The task becomes incrementally more difficult when we experience additional negative events, betrayal, and rejections that reaffirm our deeply held beliefs in our own inadequacies. Even if you are in one of the darker moments and find yourself questioning your worth, the "I am" activity is a useful tool to help gather strength and shape your reality. Our brains are capable of transforming anything when given the opportunity to do so. It isn't magic (unfortunately) and it won't happen immediately, but by creating an image of who we are or who we want to be we can start to build new neural pathways in our brains that will override the old messages and reflect our new beliefs.

I am intuitive, I am watchful. I can feel the emotions of those around me and feel it into the depths of my bones. I am the giggles of my children—the warmth in their arms. I am the fiery breath of a dragon; intimidating and fierce. I am the teardrops of my friends. My soul is fire and wine, I am never cold-blooded; I am incapable of doing anything without feeling, never indifferent. I speak from deep within my strata and boil over as fast as a pan of water on the stove. I am a priestess of the moon—powerful and alluring to those who are broken. I am in the gaze; the powerful piercing, paralyzing gaze of a cougar. I am excited before the summer storm. I am the challenging rise of the eyebrow. I am the breath and heartbeat of my sun and moon. I am the spirit and knowledge—a constant pursuit of growth and acceptance. I am the love—silent, searching and finding, and forever unbroken. I am the scars of the past—wounded, healed, reinjured and sewn back. I am the sway of the hips, shimmy of the shoulders moving to the shimmering ribbons of music—of art. I am Zahir*, in arabic meaning possessing the power to be unforgettable.

*Zahir: conceptualized by Paulo Coellho

> *"I still fall on my face sometimes,*
> *And I can't color inside the lines,*
> *Cause I'm perfectly incomplete . . .*
> *No, you haven't seen the best of me,*
> *I'm still working on my masterpiece."*
> -Jessie J. -Masterpiece

So here I am, open, vulnerable, and exposed in all of my wrinkled, frazzled, tattered, and nevertheless, beautiful glory of all that makes me, me. It is in the challenges and recovery that continue weaving the tapestry of my existence, as I build my identity of who I am and who I am choosing to become. I challenge you to see yourself through the eyes of compassion and awe of all that you have overcome, and the steps you are still taking through each transformation of life; of motherhood. There is no one version to be, nor is there a goal of what we are trying to reach when it comes to understanding and living a life reflective of your true self. Introduce yourself, be kind to whom you see within, and slowly make your way through the different aspects of all that makes you undeniably, beautifully, *You.*

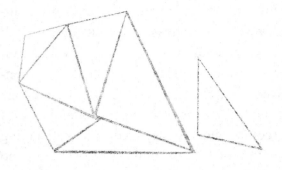

BEING MAMA

Before I had kids, I thought I had a great immune system, but it turns out that I was just really good at staying away from the type of people who sneeze directly into your eyeballs while telling you a story.

-Author Unknown

Chapter Six

Growth Usually Requires Pain

*"Everyone in my tribe has been chosen by myself
for their admirable qualities."*

Jenna Knight

www.zenfloweracu.com

fb: @JennaKAcupunctureJourney | li @jenna-knight-70585baa
t: @jknightacu

Jenna Knight

Jenna was born and raised in East Vancouver, BC, Canada. Being born into a family rich in adversity meant that she learned to fight for her health and well-being from a very early age. She completed her undergraduate studies at Thompson Rivers University, where she acquired an associate degree in a variety of studies, including health sciences, nutrition, sociology, and psychology. Jenna also completed the three-year registered acupuncturist program at the International College of Traditional Chinese Medicine (TCM) in April 2017, and wrote her licensing exams with the CTCMA in the fall of 2017.

She further expanded her studies in April 2017 by completing an internship in Taiwan at the Taipei Tzu Chi Buddhist Hospital. In the student clinic, Jenna thrived when treating the elderly, youth at risk, or individuals with emotional imbalances. Jenna has an interest in maintaining a hands-on approach, so she advanced her training in the Chinese-style massage called *Tui Na,* and completed an additional fifty hours of education in September 2017.

Jenna is a published wellness writer in *Medicinal Roots Magazine.* Jenna also contributed a chapter in *On Her Plate,* which features many young women who pride themselves on being "Wellness Warriors."

In her spare time, Jenna enjoys being in the mountains, where she explores all the beautiful hiking trails British Columbia has to offer. Here, she can take advantage of her passion for photography while also experiencing nature.

"The adventure of life is to learn. The purpose of life is to grow. The nature of life is to change." -William Arthur Ward

I'm sitting here trying to catch my breath, while thousands of thuds hit my windshield. The rain is unrelenting today, but I should expect nothing less from Vancouver weather. My pregnant belly is almost big enough to touch the steering wheel now. The slight brush of the wheel against my belly reminds my growing little one that we are still on duty for the day. I haven't had the time to emotionally grasp the idea of this surprise pregnancy; my experience has been that a blood relative will hurt you more than anyone else can, so grasping the concept of this unexpected child has torn me up inside. Not to mention that sometimes I think that this kid must think I'm crazy, since it's quite obvious that this roller-coaster ride she is on never stops moving. It's 5:00 p.m. now and we've been out of the house since 7:00 a.m., but we have to be strong because my Nana needs us tonight. I have made it through a nine-hour school day, sitting in chairs that make my pregnant body feel as though it is persisting through some kind of spinal torture treatment. My back has never hurt like this before; it's almost like my tailbone has become a dagger, which I have no choice but to sit on.

Before I start the car, I can't help but hold on to a couple of incidents from the day. First, a teacher scolded me quite firmly, letting me know I work too hard while I'm pregnant, and that because of this I will end up with a bad baby as a result. She made it sound like this would be a karmic payment I would receive for being such a terrible person. I graciously listened to her thoughts and paid her the general respect that a teacher deserves, but ultimately kept my thoughts on her cruelty to myself. I usually sit in class with a whole group of students at the back of the classroom, but they have all deserted me now, claiming that they suddenly can't see the whiteboard from this distance anymore. *I know that's a lie.* The reality is, they just don't want to sit with the only pregnant student in the classroom, who is obviously in constant discomfort. I expected better from people trying to jump into a wellness-related industry, but I am always grateful to know what a person is really made of, and being ugly on the inside is difficult to fix. These small cruelties add up slowly to create a tremendously fatigued, pregnant me. I am grateful for the experience though. I now know the burdens pregnancy can place on a woman; in the future, I can be a more empathetic, empowered female who will know when to lift up others in a similar position, rather than further pushing their energy down.

Minutes have passed, and I have spent enough time dwelling on these thoughts, so I hit the road, weary and weathered, with the sole purpose of making it to Squamish and returning home to Port Moody—a three-hour drive—all before the day's end. The road is winding and full of twists, as I hydroplane from the downpour for parts of the highway, but this doesn't seem to bother me. After the turbulent hour and a half of driving, I have made it to my Nana.

Very tentatively, I pry my puffy body out of the car seat and prepare myself, both mentally and physically, that I need to be the caregiver for my Nana now. Like a switch, I turn my emotions off and make her my priority. I know this magical switch is a coping mechanism, a skill that I can use to create internal resilience. My childhood years may have been treacherous at best, but they gave me these tools that I can pull out of my metaphorical toolbox to use now when I'm struggling as an adult. I was only able to acquire these tools because I was willing and capable of seeing lessons while living in what I call *explosive darkness.* For this reason, I feel extreme gratitude for being able to experience all of my past hardships.

Out of the car, I shift my tired gaze up and make eye contact with my grandmother. I can see that there is very little of her left in this body now. It is as if I look into hollow eyes; the lights are on, but her spirit is mostly gone. I know she won't live to see the birth of my first and only baby, and I'm severely aware of the fact that I have no family to help me navigate being a new mother. But I put these emotions that are starting to turn into a tornado of pain aside because in this moment, it's not about me. I am the only one who can help her now; my Nana has sworn me to secrecy about the severity of her situation; no one else in our family knows she is terminally ill. She just can't chance a highly addicted family member bringing unnecessary drama to the side of her deathbed. Or the persistence of the money-hungry ones who will hound her for every last penny she still owns. So, like a dungeon, I lock away the weight of such a secret and carry on with my duties.

My visit is over, everything that needed to be done is done, and yet I don't feel accomplished, happy, or even satisfied. Right now, it's all about keeping her comfortable and planning for death. The idea of planning for death feels like submitting an assignment, the most important assignment of your life, all while perfectly understanding that no matter what you write, you will fail. Because in the end, there is still a loss, grief, death, and a void within your heart that will never be filled. At this point, I'm feeling distressed by the fact that I have become very familiar with the scent associated with death; this pregnant state has heightened my sense of smell to the point where, if this were a contest, I could give a bloodhound a run for its money. The scent of tissue cells about to die frolics in the air, like a feather dancing on a light breeze. On top of this, I've been given the task of carrying out my grandmother's last wishes, as she continues to make me promise to keep her health problems a secret. It feels heavy; breathing almost feels like a chore. Yet my sense of duty is somewhat like a fictitious whip that makes my feet continue to move, even when I feel crushed by this life.

I make it home, back to Port Moody; it's 10:00 p.m. My husband looks at me with amazement—that as a pregnant woman, between full-time studies and caring for my Nana, I have made it through another fifteen-hour, on-your-feet kind of day. I do this crazy routine at least three days a week, while also holding a part-time job. Although, I know that I cannot move at even a fraction of the level of my usual productivity while at work. For me, it's normal to move so quickly, it may seem like I'm dancing circles around everyone else. This is supposed to be one of the happiest times in my life, but I don't have a magical Disney movie unfolding around me. This doesn't get to me, though, as duty and responsibility are extremely important to my core beliefs.

I feel my circle of support decreasing in circumference, and as my due date creeps up on me, I'm ever more aware that I have no family to call upon. Slowly but surely, my time for the big show is coming. I wasn't emotionally prepared to be a full-time student while also coping with a surprise pregnancy. Now my grandmother, who is my best friend, my constant cheerleader, my guardian angel on this earth, and my only close family member, is going to die. I haven't even been given a chance to grieve for my father-in-law, who passed away after a heroic battle with leukemia the year before. All of this has made me feel, for the first time, that this life is just not fair. I used to resent people who felt this way, but now I get it. I can't afford to dwell on negative thoughts, though, so I persevere and make the best out of each day, using the concept of being a person with strong intestinal fortitude, a trait my Nana had always praised me on, for having been given a strong dose of it. Reflecting on these small memories of my time with my Nana brings slight smiles to my face, which are hard to come by these days.

It's time for bed, which is supposed to be restful but at this point, it's more like practicing continuous contortion in an attempt to find a comfortable position. It feels like it's always dark around me now; the rain is everlasting and leaves me in a pool of gloom. My husband and I try to find a few minutes to connect, but with such a small window for love, it has become difficult. I know that he is elated about this pregnancy, but I have not yet accepted the surprise. He wears the guilt all over his tired face; his heart knows he asked me to keep a baby I never planned on having. For now, though, we can't work on all our concerns; there is simply too much on our plate. So we come together as a team, working in unison toward the common goal of being in a loving relationship that can overcome all of life's turbulent periods.

It's the start of another school day. I feel like death, and I'm sure I look like it, too, as the commentary has already started to pour in for the day. Today I'm told to take a break from my grandmother, which I know I can't accept. I know if I needed help, my grandmother would crawl through the Sahara Desert with two broken legs to save me, so in her time of need at the ripe age of 101, I must come to her aid and be there for her as much as I can. Such a silly comment brings me to believe that the person making it cannot fathom the idea of putting another human being before themselves. The almost constant comments about my pregnancy and health are so unnecessary; they make me feel misunderstood and add no value to my day, just more stress and more practice at maintaining my poised composure. Though I am constantly surrounded by people, I often feel alone. The negativity has turned an extroverted, social butterfly like me into an individual who just wants distance.

I can see that this is a recipe for emotional disaster, so I have set a firm intention that my baby will have every ounce of my energy needed to be healthy and happy. I am strong enough to make do with whatever life force is left after I have given this girl everything she could possibly need, and then some. I take it a step further and envision a steel, dome-shaped birdcage protecting my little girl, like an impenetrable Eden. Whenever another comment is flung at me like mud, I focus my energy on filling the inside of this Eden with bright light and love, shielding both my own and my little girl's life force and energy. All the negativity stays on the outside; within me, there is nothing but pure love. I practice this intention routine daily and feel every nudge and kick, as she responds to me thinking of her with nothing but love, affection, and protection.

As my grandmother dwindles away, taking my only support with her, it is painfully obvious to me that this is going to be a problem, and I must make it a priority to cultivate a tribe of people to help me if needed. A close friend reminds me that it takes a village to raise a child; I'm so used to negativity by now that I almost don't know how to respond to such a positive and useful comment. It takes me a second to digest what exactly she means, and then the inspiration hits me. I use her comment as a metaphorical push to reach out in my community and acquire any resources, information, or guidance that I may need; to use once our little one is here.

The warmth continues at school, which surprises me beyond belief; a mentor makes a thoughtful comment that brings light back into my eyes. She knows that this baby is a surprise and senses I'm uneasy about the experience. I'm sure it's easy to see this uneasiness in my wild eyes and rapid breathing, almost like a horse about to be broken. She tells me that I should not worry, for this journey will be beautiful and when my soul leaves this world, it will leave feeling full, having had every experience a human can have in this lifetime. This conversation hits me in the heart; she will never know how much I appreciated her kindness at this moment. It was as if for just a few seconds, she filled in as my adoptive mother and gave me the kindness I had struggled to find from anyone each day.

With this positive energy, I go a step further now and protect my mental health by seeing a counselor on a weekly basis. This counselor is lovely and provides me with an outlet, where nothing is expected from me other than to accept her support. Most of the time, she is completely flabbergasted by my perseverance, determination, and sense of duty; at times, I leave her speechless. I mentally add her to my tribe of people from whom I can acquire information, skills, and guidance. Most people have family they can call upon when they are in need. I have become okay with the idea that my tribe consists of a list of people whom I, myself, have sourced. I accept this as a positive—everyone in my tribe has been chosen by me for their admirable qualities, whereas in the case of family, it is not a choice.

I make it my priority to boost my physical health by acquiring acupuncture treatments on a weekly basis as well. Being an acupuncturist myself, I know these treatments will help balance my mind, body, and soul, while also giving me the endurance I still need to make it through this last semester of school, work, and caring for my Nana before she passes. These acupuncture treatments are like a God-send; nothing is required from me during this time, so I can focus on nothing more than replenishing my well-being as a whole. As I lay on the treatment table, heavy with exhaustion, it is as if my body has become part of the bed. I feel every nudge, every bit of gratitude my little one expresses internally, thanking me for taking care of myself: her mom.

* * *

I know from my education and according to traditional Chinese medicine, pregnancy is considered a very special time in a woman's life. The idea is that during this time, there will be an abundance of *Yin* energy within the body, as a woman does not menstruate or bleed regularly for the duration of the pregnancy. There will be a steady, gradual increase in fluids as the little person inside of a woman starts to grow. This can be a huge strain on a mother because the woman's life force is used to nourish her growing child; we call this life force *Essence*. Essence diminishes as we age, becoming depleted slowly until we pass away to the next life. It is said that this life force is stored in the kidneys, and so the kidneys' energy, known as *Qi*, is also partially depleted during pregnancy. In addition, in traditional Chinese medicine, we expect that the Liver, *Chong*, and *Ren* meridians will experience partial consumption by the entire process of housing and growing a little person.

As an acupuncturist and from my own personal experience, I can clearly see the immense benefits that can be grasped and utilized for pregnant women. Treatments can be used to nourish the blood, to help the pregnant mother with the obvious and tremendous demand for healthy blood. Acupuncture points can be chosen to benefit the Kidney meridian and Essence at the same time, to supplement a woman's overall life force. The body's energy can be moved gently to prevent further health issues, and acupuncture treatments can also be used to improve digestion for optimum gastrointestinal health and nutrient absorption. In traditional Chinese medicine, we view the Stomach and Spleen as primary organs related to blood production. Treatment for pregnant women can be focused on boosting the Spleen to benefit the blood. Because we have such a variety of acupuncture points available to choose from, each individual's needs can be met in different ways. My studies, although burdening my mind with more effort, have given me a temporary escape from the stresses of my sick grandmother.

As time passes and the days pile up, we are now very close to my Nana drifting away into the next world. I make every effort to be with her so that she will not have to die alone. She can't speak anymore; only small sounds of gibberish come out as she struggles to communicate. It seems that she doesn't recognize anyone either—except for me, of course. When I enter the room, her soft eyes light up just a little bit, and her frail arms reach out to hold me. I know that I am her favorite person in this world, just as intensely as she is mine. Her sounds make no sense, but I know exactly what she is trying to say—she doesn't want to pass away and leave this world because she is worried about me. I gently hold her hand as if she is so delicate that she may break and hush her worries, giving her as much comfort as I can. I don't cry when I am with her, even though everyone else in the room is bawling. I know that any sadness on my face will alarm her more than she already is, and at this time in her life, I will not add to her suffering. So I stay strong and give her nothing but love.

The next day, she falls asleep and does not wake up. The relief is immediate—it is as though the weight of the Empire State Building has come off my shoulders. I can breathe again, and I know that her suffering is over, which eases me to no end. Now that her physical body is gone, I know the effort she felt from forcing life past its expiry is over, and now her soul can float effortlessly, like a feather in the wind. Even though she is gone, I will take every lesson she has given me and apply those teachings to my day-to-day life so that in turn, her Essence will live on through me.

With this one idea coursing through my thoughts, I realize that I am, in fact, not alone in raising my daughter. My grandmother has taught me everything I need to know just by having me care for her in her final months and days of life. She gave me the opportunity to care for someone in their most vulnerable state. She taught me to be an advocate for an individual who could not voice their own needs or care for themselves in any capacity. She taught me to be strong and pull energy out of my being, even when I was far beyond my point of total depletion, so that I could provide good care to someone other than myself. My grandmother gave me the ability to give nothing but love, support, protection, and kindness to another individual when there was no possible gain for me other than fulfilling my duty as a granddaughter. For all these reasons and more, my grandmother taught me to be a great mother, in the most indirect fashion possible and for that, I bow to her spirit with gratitude.

Resources:

- *The Essential Guide To Acupuncture in Pregnancy & Childbirth*, by Debra Betts
- *Diagnosis in Chinese Medicine: A Comprehensive Guide*, by Giovanni Maciocia
- *Obstetrics and Gynecology in Chinese Medicine*, by Giovanni Maciocia
- *The Foundations of Chinese Medicine*, by Giovanni Maciocia; page 44-45, 69, 155, 229-230, 268, 349, and 593
- *The Channels of Acupuncture,* by Giovanni Maciocia; chapter 24-28
- *Diagnosis in Chinese Medicine,* by Giovanni Maciocia; page 406-408, 837, and 842

Chapter Seven

Our GA1 Warrior: The Journey of a Medically Compromised Little Girl

*"To show our children they too can be
unstoppable is the ultimate gift."*

Valerie Steele

val@birjareno.ca

ig: @steelebirja | fb: @valeriesteele | t: @valerie849

Valerie Steele

Valerie Steele has an adventurous and determined spirit. She has spent the majority of her life seeking the unfamiliar. Whether through gorilla trekking in Rwanda, white-water rafting along the Nile, hiking Cinque Terre's coastal trails, practicing yoga in Nepal, or biking through Tuscany, these experiences have all illuminated her heart with gratitude. She enjoys the beauty of nature and journaling. She is a teacher by trade and a writer by heart. Valerie's late grandmother instilled the love of books and reading in her as a child. She has had a number of her articles published in local newspapers.

Valerie is a graduate of the University of Guelph and the University of Ottawa. She is passionate about empowering girls and women. Valerie truly believes you can do anything that you set your mind to, which she mastered from her amazing parents. Their positive and selfless support is unwavering and she is forever thankful. Valerie believes that adversity can also bring opportunity. She has taught middle school students for fourteen years. Before becoming an intermediate level teacher, she taught horseback riding lessons for many years to adults and children with special needs. She has also taught at a teacher's college in China, traveled to India, Nepal, Kenya, Uganda, Denmark, and various other countries. Valerie now lives in Heartlake, Ontario, Canada with her husband and daughter, with the dream of showing her daughter the beauty of the world.

"You gain strength, courage and confidence by every experience in which you really stop to look fear in the face. You must do the thing which you think you cannot do."
-Eleanor Roosevelt

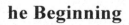he Beginning

The sun rays beamed through my car windows as I drove along the country roads, it was surreal to think that I was finally driving to my baby shower. Attending more showers than I could count, a feeling of warm gratitude came over me. As I looked down at my mighty belly, I imagined who this little person might become and what it would be like, once I became a mother. At that moment, I pictured everything from mom and baby yoga classes, library programs, to swimming classes, and little did I know that the Universe had other plans for us. Our parenting preparation checklist and prenatal classes could not have prepared us on how to become parents of a child with a rare metabolic condition.

The reality I experienced as a new mother was very different than the one I had envisioned. In a society that always pushes us to consume more protein, we have spent the entirety of our daughter's life avoiding it. I had a healthy pregnancy without any complications. Our incredible daughter was born on August 19th, 2016 at 5:59 p.m. Overwhelmed with emotion and exhaustion, we could not believe that we were holding our perfect baby girl. She passed all the routine tests and examinations with flying colors.

For six days, we thought we had a typical healthy baby. For six days, we had the usual concerns of new parents. Is our baby latching and feeding enough? Is our baby too cold or too hot?

We watched our precious baby girl's chest rise and fall every time she slept, and felt relief with every sound. We examined every little facial feature and knew she was our beautiful miracle. It was the most fierce, and protective love I have ever experienced. Then on day six, that phone call came from our doctor. It changed our lives forever. All I remember hearing on the other end was what our doctor said, "Your daughter has been diagnosed with a rare genetic disease that could affect her brain." I immediately started crying and she said not to do so, or my milk supply would stop. She then told me she had already contacted my husband and that he was on his way home from work to pick us up. We were instructed to take our daughter to the emergency room at Sick Kids Hospital right away as the metabolic department was expecting us. The drive was the longest, most silent, and fearsome journey I've ever experienced. My husband's eyes met mine, and I knew we would do whatever it took to protect our baby girl, but we felt terrified.

Newborn Screening Saved Her Life

At the emergency, a team of people took our daughter and began poking and prodding her. I remember being in a little room, flooded with geneticists, dietitians, metabolic doctors, and nurses. I was a mess and felt so helpless. I prayed it was a false positive. They quickly explained to us that they wanted to run some more tests to confirm a diagnosis for a rare metabolic condition called Glutaric Aciduria/Acidemia Type 1 (GA1). In the first twenty-four hours of life, all babies in Ontario are screened for GA1, along with twenty-eight other diseases.[1]

I had never even heard of newborn screening (NBS). Although I had no idea what it was, specifically, I do remember that nurse

1   Newborn Screening Ontario. 2017. Accessed month day, year. http://www.newbornscreening.ca

who took a drop of blood from my baby girl's heel after she was born, right before we brought her home for the first time. It was through NBS that my daughter's condition was diagnosed, and it saved her life. Newborn screening saves thousands of lives every year, and I'm thankful every single day for this indescribable gift. It is the process of testing newborn babies for some serious, but treatable conditions. The conditions newborn babies are screened for varies depending on province or state. According to Newborn Screening Ontario, hospitals now screen for twenty-nine diseases including metabolic diseases, cystic fibrosis, sickle cell anemia, PKU, and endocrine diseases. Babies with one of the tested diseases appear normal at birth, and without newborn screening, might not be identified before irreversible damage has occurred. Most of these babies will not have a family history of the disease. My husband and I are both carriers of GA1, but we had no idea.

We quickly learned that early identification of the disease allows treatment that can prevent severely devastating outcomes. It was challenging to find anything positive on the internet, but I kept searching and searching. It was one of the most difficult times in my life. I wanted to just curl up into a tiny ball, but I knew my daughter needed us to learn as much as possible. Children with GA1 who do not receive early treatment via NBS, most often suffer a crisis, also known as a metabolic stroke, which would leave these angels in a wheelchair and typically non-verbal. Before GA1 was discovered in the late 1990s, it was believed to be late onset cerebral palsy or also referred to as "locked-in syndrome." Fortunately, there is now technology such as the eyegaze system, to help these children communicate as they are all cognitively functioning at one hundred percent. All the families affected by GA1 are amazing warriors, battling the unknown, and sometimes what feels like the impossible. The research for this rare disease stops at six years old. After that, we celebrate graduating out of the high-risk zone and continue to monitor every single illness. From three months to thirty-six months is the highest risk for a GA1 child to have a metabolic stroke to the brain, also known as a crisis. We do everything in our power to avoid this, which could be triggered by something as common as a fever. These children are my superheroes, and these mama warriors are the ones who inspire me. Fortunately, there is a Facebook support group where we can follow each other's journeys, joys, challenges, and most importantly, lift each other up in the moments we need it most. These mothers from all over the world are connecting, supporting, and rising up to be there for one another. The day I found this online support group, I felt a sense of hope and it changed my world.

Live In Love, Not Fear

After our daughter's diagnosis was confirmed, she was admitted to Sick Kids Hospital, Toronto, where we were given a "crash course" on what GA1 was, and the guidelines we had to follow to keep her healthy. We knew we had to avoid viruses at all costs. The next day, we were supposed to be taking her to our first family get together, which was now a threat to our baby girl. Everyone we knew had little kids who are like petri dishes of germs. Her immune system is perfectly fine, but when a child with GA1 gets a cold, their bodies don't work as well. Children with metabolic conditions are often medically fragile. It was a tough time for us after our daughter's diagnosis. It was a turbulent ride going back and forth between exhaustion from sleeping at the hospital, to shock, to dealing with postpartum hormones, and then grief. My vision, of what I envisioned motherhood to be, had been completely altered.

The real challenge was to remain positive, hopeful, and powerful in the middle of it all. Often, our automatic panic button is in overdrive, and we can be swept away by fear. I was definitely in a complete state of fear, and blinked-back tears as the doctors continued to explain that people with metabolic conditions have a defective gene that results in an enzyme deficiency. I asked them if there was a cure, and how rare it is, and he let me know that one in one hundred thousand children are affected, and that this is a condition she will have for life. Sick Kids Hospital had two other cases of GA1. It hit me like a lightning bolt, despite how helpless I felt, I had to learn as much as I could to protect my daughter. I soaked up all the information like a sponge and became obsessed with trying to understand it all. My daughter's body can't break down protein properly. Specifically, her body is unable to break down the amino acids lysine, hydroxylysine, and tryptophan.[2]

As a result, a toxic substance of glutaric acid builds up in her body, which could cause a stroke to the basal ganglia part of her brain. She is at high risk of having a metabolic stroke at any sign of illness until she is three years of age. The common cold could put her in the hospital. The risk decreases significantly once she turns six-years-old, as that part of the brain is fully developed. However, there are still so many unknowns about this condition as it has only been considered treatable since 2006.

Our New Reality

I had multiple questions swirling around in my mind at full speed. What if I make a mistake? How am I going to do this? What if I fail? I think a lot of parenting is about believing in your

---

2   GARD. 2017. "Glutaric acidemia type 1." National Center for Advancing Translational Sciences. Accessed month day, year. https://rarediseases.info.nih.gov/diseases/6522/glutaric-acidemia-type-i

abilities and trusting that you've got this. I learned that it's not about what happens to us, but how we choose to respond. Often, adversity will be an opportunity to gain a new perspective if you allow it. I tried to remind myself that out of great difficulties, there can be miracles. I also thought that I would be the person to show and teach my daughter how to be brave and believe in herself. I was wrong. In fact, it is she who has taught me these things on a whole new level.

She began her medications at six-days-old and takes them three times a day, and even though she's only sixteen-months-old, she takes them herself like a champ. She will be on these meds for life, along with a protein (lysine) restricted diet and special medical formula. We measure everything on a scale. It's complicated because pretty much everything we eat has protein in it. Even watermelon has protein and needs to be measured so she doesn't consume too much lysine. Most important is the illness management protocol, which involves IV fluids at any sign of illness, fever, diarrhea, or lack of appetite. The IV fluids provide extra sugars and hydration, both of which are vital to protect her brain. This prevents her body from breaking down her own protein when the demand for energy has increased. Preventing this catabolic state is what prevents the toxins from building up in her brain. She has had weekly appointments at Sick Kids Hospital for blood work, and now they are every couple of months. Her most recent hospitalization involved eight attempts before finding a final IV spot. My daughter inspires me so much and her bravery makes me stronger. She has been through a lot, but continues to radiate endless love and light. Every time we are there, I ask myself, *what can I do to protect her more? What should I be advocating for right now?* It's often hard for me to fully trust the doctors and nurses. None of us are experts in GA1. It's the absolute epitome of lifelong learning. Right now, she can have four grams of protein a day. We have to keep daily logs of her food and medical formula intake. Luckily, as she grows older, her protein allowance will increase. These are all positives as they keep our daughter safe. She is thriving and it definitely keeps us moving forward.

Strength From My Soul Sisters And Mothers

I have learned to live in love and not fear. It definitely took some time, as I had to mourn certain expectations and learn to embrace this new journey. The day my daughter was diagnosed, my husband inspired me by saying, "We will not let GA1 defeat us and we need to shower away any negativity or fear." That is just what we did and we have survived so much together this past year. My own incredible mother also gave me powerful advice when I was feeling less than confident to handle everything. She said, "You can do this because she's your daughter and you are her protector." I began to focus on what could go right rather than the things that could go wrong. Although very few people understood this rare condition, I felt compelled to explain this rare condition to anyone who would listen. I was very fortunate and had a few friends who indeed got it. They helped by checking in, listening, and reminding me to stay positive. These friends are also incredible mothers and I will forever be grateful for their support when I needed it most. A special thank you to my friend Tia, who was our very first visitor during our first hospitalization. I remember the nurses telling me someone was waiting at the registration desk. I wondered who it was, and as I slowly walked out of isolation, I saw my incredibly thoughtful and selfless good friend, Tia. It brought tears to my eyes and I will forever remember that hug because I have never needed one more. She couldn't come and see my daughter because we were in isolation, but she left us with some homemade muffins and hope. She reminded me that we were in an incredible place surrounded by miracles. As mothers and women warriors, we all need to connect and embrace each other during the challenges of this journey called motherhood. Not only is it about reframing our thinking or rediscovering feelings that empower and uplift us. We need to reach out to others to help guide us, teach us, and then take these lessons and share them with others. I genuinely believe the Universe is always working for us and if we learn to listen to the subtle signs, then we are reminded that we are not alone. We need to lean on each other, inspire each other, and empower one another. This is what can show our children that they too can be unstoppable and resilient in the face of adversity. There are villages of mama warriors that surround us, and I believe that there's always an opportunity that can be discovered from a difficult situation.

Raising A Medically Fragile Child

Adjusting to this new lifestyle of raising a medically fragile child has definitely been a process. It means we have decided to avoid taking her to public places where people are often sick. Daycare is not an option. Neither are airplanes or traveling right now. Our daughter has never been to a mall, a grocery store, or a public play space. We prefer to socialize outdoors with her, but cold and flu season is the scariest. We sanitize constantly and hand hygiene is of utmost importance to us. We had to miss Christmas and other various family get-togethers because of someone having a cold or some virus. Being new parents and having to avoid family and friends due to illness constantly can be very isolating.

When my husband or I are feeling unwell, we wear a mask at all times, or leave home and stay somewhere else, until we are no longer a threat to our daughter. Playdates can be dangerous as toddlers are often carriers of viruses even when they appear well. Birthday parties are a challenge.

She's allowed four grams of protein a day and all of her food has to be measured continuously. Birthday cake, pizza, and ice cream all have too much protein for her to have right now. Despite these new ways of living, I am eternally grateful and humbled to know my daughter has a chance to live a normal and healthy life.

Despite all of our precautions, she has had nine hospitalizations in the first year of her life because of illness. These were extremely emotional and hard, but visitors always put a smile on our faces. My sister always reminds me that our daughter is a fighter and has been an amazing source of support. My daughter is a happy, healthy, and strong toddler who lights up every room she is in. Life with a rare condition is a unique journey, and her determined spirit and fearless nature makes us braver and more hopeful with each new moment. However, raising a medically fragile child has you constantly thinking about what germs you are possibly bringing home. If I have been in a crowded public place, I will shower and change my clothes before holding my daughter. We sanitize our phones and wash our hands immediately upon entering the house. Everyone that comes over must not have been around anyone sick, and have to wash their hands and sanitize before touching our daughter. Our family doctor always lets our daughter have the first appointment of the day to avoid sick people. The metabolic doctors are on speed dial in case of illness twenty-four hours a day. This is life with a medically fragile child, and I wouldn't change it for the world. Motherhood has shown me what I am capable of, and being able to nurture our daughter's progress is pure magic. Every single day and every second with our daughter is a gift. She is our bright light and little GA1 warrior who reminds us to be fearless in the face of adversity and to dance every day.

Unstoppable

Every milestone she achieves magnifies our gratitude, our joy, and our hopes. Every day that she spends at home and away from the hospital is a victory. Each moment she laughs and engages with another child without getting sick is a relief. Looking into my daughter's innocent eyes, I can see her fierce determination and her unstoppable spirit which makes all of this possible. Her power is confidence, her power is resilience, and her power is love. I strive to be present and grateful in every moment, which is not always easy. I try to remember to embrace every single second of motherhood because often, we feel so exhausted and lose the ability to be present. We accomplish what needs to be done and we live in love rather than fear. To feel powerful when faced with adversity can take time and healing. One of the doctors gave me great advice. She said, "You need to remember to enjoy your baby." In that moment, I realized that I was so consumed with my daughter's meds, diet, illness management protocols, and how many bottles of medical formula she had consumed in a day, that I forgot to let myself live and be present within each beautiful and messy moment as a new mother. I was given this remarkable gift and needed to treasure every single day.

I have this fantastic opportunity to watch my child grow. Whether motherhood carries excitement, joy, sorrow, painful decisions, tender love, or confusion, it is our destiny. It is my purpose to keep our angel safe, advocate for our little GA1 warrior, and to educate the world about her rare needs. Whether you can relate to my journey or not, we were all given a unique treasure. Motherhood isn't always glamorous, but we need to continue to be our children's protectors, advocates, and their blankets of love. To show them that they too can be unstoppable and can do anything is the ultimate gift we can give them. The possibilities are endless and there is this love we feel with every fiber of our being for our child. It is the most motivating and powerful force that can give us a strength we didn't even know we had.

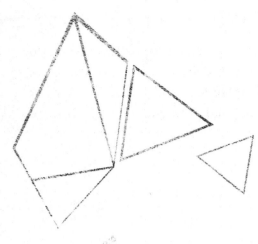

BEING MAMA

I let my kids follow their dreams. Unless I already paid the registration fee on their last dream. Then they follow that for another eight weeks.

@generation.mom

Chapter Eight

I'm Back . . . Boss Mama in the Big Apple

"I knew it was time to clean up from a beautiful time in my life and move on to a new year and a new adventure. It was time for me, again, to trust the magic of new beginnings."

Erica Lambert

ericalambertlifestyle.com | champagnecopywriting.com

ig: @ericalambertlifestyle | @sparkleeverydayblog_
@champagnecopywriting
fb: @ericalambertlifestyle | @champagnecopywriting

Erica Lambert

Erica Lambert is a motivational lifestyle blogger, wedding writer, and mommy of two boys: Leo, two and Fox, one. Her writing career started in the wedding industry for the romance of it all, but she soon discovered life itself offers a romance all its own. It is full of love and adventure—in its own way, in its own time. Erica lives along the white sandy beaches of Northwest Florida, on the panhandle, and currently manages her lifestyle blog, Erica Lambert Lifestyle, and her boutique copywriting house for wedding professionals, Champagne Copywriting. In her down time, she enjoys riding bikes with her husband along the beach, sipping champagne at brunch with friends, and playing with her two boys outside by the sea.

Being an entrepreneur, and a working mama in general, in many ways means being willing and open to change; change in focus, change in direction, and change in lifestyle. When you become a mama you find that change isn't always welcomed, in most cases, mine included. Creating a world with minimal change is the only way of survival from week to week with little ones. Conquering the act of wearing two crowns with varying skills and expectations is the key to creating the life you have always wanted—from loving, raising, and cheering on your little ones in the things they love to do, and cheering yourself on and pushing for greatness in accomplishing your personal and professional goals.

Ever since I was a little girl . . . I've dreamed of living in New York City. I would imagine the sound of my heels clicking on the sidewalk as I walked to my dream job. My days would be filled with creative brainstorming sessions, editorial calendars, cocktails with friends, and an uptown apartment.

Being from a small town in Alabama, I didn't think this dream was super realistic. I love that I grew up in a small southern town, though sometimes I think it may have altered my views on the world and societal norms. My strong moral values and desire to surround myself with family was crafted by living in a small town. However, growing up, it seemed like a lot of women my mom's age who had children, let go of their professional aspirations (if any) to be moms, and housewives. The apple didn't fall far from the tree when their daughters would enter beauty pageants, and one-by-one would say (when asked what their biggest goal in life was) "to get married and raise babies." While there is nothing wrong with this, I personally found it unappealing.

I was someone who would daydream in class all through elementary school, high school, and college about what I wanted to be when I grew up, which only made me feel like an outcast to my peers. I often felt alone for wanting to have a creative career path that was considered out-of-the box. Creativity was always something I felt passionate about and wanted to talk about, but it never seemed of interest to my peers in high school, so I internalized it.

I felt like I would pursue things, research things, and the things I was supposed to do and see what stood out to me. I never really had anyone in my family, group of friends or college counselors to turn to for specific career advice in the creative industries I was interested in. So, I did my own research. Most of the time, my research would end in countless nights of feeling like my dreams (whatever they were) would never come to fruition. The city seemed to stifle creativity, and there were few opportunities for creative growth. But I was determined to make it happen. I had no idea how, but one day I knew I would live in New York City. Once in college, I remember my advisor trying to push me away from being involved in weddings as a career choice. She and the university I attended had a connection to the Disney internship program. They wanted all of their students to consider applying. As wonderful as Disney is to visit, this program was not appealing to me. With that, I pivoted. I changed the concentration of my studies in business from hospitality and tourism to marketing, which turned out to be the best decision for me.

Industry-specific Facebook groups were not as big as they are now if they existed at all. So I hustled to find anyone who would teach me more about the wedding industry. The romance and glamor of weddings always made my eyes sparkle. That is how I knew I was going in the right direction! I was obsessed with finding wedding-related or event planning jobs close to me. Turns out the wedding industry is filled with other hustlers. So and So's event planning was basically a one-person show. Needless to say, even finding an internship was far from easy. That was until I struck gold my senior year. I landed a fantastic internship with an event planning company in NYC! The internship was through a program I had applied for, months before. I wasn't expecting much from the submission until I received an acceptance email!

From there I interviewed over-the-phone with several companies in Manhattan, each having specific needs. The internship I went with was one that needed content creation, blog writing, and social media management. Since I changed my major to marketing, I knew this would be perfect for me!

The best part of creating content for an event planning company was getting to go to all the events to write about them! About two months into the three-month internship, I started to enjoy writing blog posts about wedding trends and wedding-related events in the city. I loved it, actually.

On a random day, I received an email invitation to a Rent the Runway event at XO Group, which I came to find out was home to none other than The Knot, The Bump, and The Nest. The event was about women empowerment and women in business, which was so my thing! The office I worked out of every day was downtown on Fulton Street. After a quick Google search, turns out the XO Group offices were also on Fulton—easy!

Right after work, I spruced up my hair a bit, re-applied my red lipstick, and walked one block over. I wasn't exactly sure what XO Group was to be honest, but once in the building and in the elevator, each floor became more and more exciting. The doors opened two levels below the floor I was headed to. Someone stepped out and walked toward the giant letters that read HarperCollins, which hung above a busy reception desk.

Next stop, XO Group. The elevator doors opened to the lobby with giant glass doors with XO Group: The Knot, The Bump, and The Nest written on the main entrance. THE KNOT! I had a minor fangirl moment (on the inside) before walking into the offices. I was greeted by two girls put together as if they had gotten dressed in Blair Waldorf's closet before heading to work (love!). They were so sweet and welcoming as they guided me down to where the event was being held. On the way to the event, we passed rows and rows of Mac desktops, atop pristine white desks, which were surrounded by floor to ceiling glass windows overlooking the sparkling city lights. As I walked further, I noticed walls and walls of small magazine pages assembled to perfection, color schemes, and a whiteboard with trending wedding topics written at the top.

Then it hit me. I was in the editorial department. My dream department in my dream city, right there in front of my eyes. I continue walking, and a girl swings open the door to pull out a rolling rack of couture wedding gowns. As I walked past her, I was able to sneak a peek at the fashion closet, which was clearly what every glamor-loving girl would live for.

Before arriving at the large room overlooking the lights of the city and the Brooklyn Bridge, I said to myself: this is it! This is where I want to work, and I will make it happen somehow. I had zero ideas where to even start to get to that point, but almost two years later, an opportunity presented itself.

I got an email from a co-worker from my internship. She was the full-time events coordinator on staff, and I reported directly to her. She wrote to tell me about how she had moved on from the event planning company to work at, no other than, The Knot. After a burst of excitement for her and a twinge of jealousy (maybe more than a twinge), she told me she was working in a new department where she matched brides to venues for their wedding day.

She had remembered my talking about the event I attended at XO Group that summer and how much it affected me to my core. Turns out, there was a job opening she thought I would be interested in . . . and of course I was! I interviewed, got the job, and put out a message in my old NYU internship program Facebook page.

Funnily enough, a friend I had made while interning responded that she was also looking for a roommate for around the same move-in date. If you can't tell by now, the universe was all over me moving to New York the way things started to align so perfectly.

It was springtime in New York City when I flew into Laguardia airport with four pieces of luggage and excitement in my heart. After my internship, I wondered if I would ever be back to finish what I started. And there I was, standing in the middle of Union Square. "I'm back," I said out loud. Part of me couldn't believe it as I stood there looking around my old familiar neighborhood. Nothing really changed since the last time I was living there. Except for maybe the national debt counter displayed on one of the buildings in Union Square. It had gone up quite a bit in a year or so.

When thinking of myself just up and moving to the city alone to pursue a passion, I've often felt courageous. But when I think of my move back to Florida, I feel like people (and maybe even myself for a while) viewed that as a failure. I had no real plan when moving back home to Santa Rosa Beach, I just felt a massive pull in that direction. I didn't know exactly why, but I knew it was the right decision. Now I know my why for moving, and I feel 1000% that I am where I should be. I don't think my story is that of what a movie script would lead you to believe—the girl who moved to follow her dreams, landed the dream job and lived happily ever after. I think MY story is that of the journey of finding myself and just going for it. Following my gut.

The decision to leave NYC was just as complicated and scary to make as moving there in the first place, if not harder. What the hell was I going to do after leaving my "dream" job? Was I making the biggest mistake of my life? Would people think I left my career for love (remember my fiancé back home in Florida)? Would I forever be viewed as "that" girl? The one who let her dreams die? The one who let a man decide her fate? But it was none of those things. There was a pull in my heart to go back home, yes, but my major anxiety played a huge part in me making the difficult decision.

The moment I packed my bags and bought a one-way ticket to work at the wedding magazine I'd swooned over for years, is the moment I feel like people thought, "Wow, she did it. She made it." But to me, my moment was making the blind move to self-discovery.

Not only recognizing for the first time how debilitating my anxiety could be and how it played such a huge role in my life—not always for the best. Plus, knowing my intuition was telling me something and listening. I would never have known the things I know now about myself had I stayed in the city I love so much.

I've always prided myself on my ability to follow my intuition and trust what the universe has in store for me. But I also had a nasty case of crippling anxiety stemming from me not feeling pretty enough, smart enough, fancy enough, or good enough on any level to align with the aspirations I had for myself.

And sure enough, after the "new" started to wear off New York, I slowly began to feel the anxiety creep in. I had been able to keep it at bay by enjoying the newness of the city, but soon it would take over my life again. I was self-conscious about my southern accent and afraid people would stereotype me into something I'm not. Suddenly I found myself hiding all of the unique things about myself.

I had constructed this story in my mind, that no one at work thought I should be there at all. That irrational feeling made me question every single move I made. I started to feel my confidence slip. I stopped looking people in the eye and kept to myself. From the start, I was excited to pick out my outfits, accessories, and heels to wear to work. Then I slowly started dressing down to keep people from looking my way.

I stopped wearing heels because the sheer thought of walking to the restroom overwhelmed me with anxiety. My heels would click on the marble floor, and I would feel people looking at me. No one was ever looking at me like "omg this girl and her heels again, they were merely glancing at the noise approaching them."

I had created this entire story in my head that people were judging me for the exact same thing they were wearing! All the girls, including myself, would wear more comfortable clothes and closed-toe shoes to work due to the subway being such a production every day.

Since I was traveling from uptown to downtown, my commute was about an hour and some change there, and the same on my way home . . . on a good day. Once at work, we would change into our chic and professional clothes, apply a dab of lipstick, grab a cup of coffee and breakfast from the kitchen, and start our workday. I got along with everyone, made friends, and genuinely enjoyed the work I was doing, but I had it made up in my mind that I was not worthy of being there.

Suddenly it was Winter in New York and I was so excited to see snow—finally. Real snow. Not just flurries that rarely stick to the ground like in Alabama. It was a Saturday when the first big snow occurred—winter storm Juno. I remember thinking how magical it would be to sip my morning coffee, looking out onto the snow-filled streets. With that thought, I put on my warmest clothes and headed downstairs. Right before opening the doors to the stoop, I paused thinking *how beautiful!* It looked just like a snow globe! Then . . . I opened the doors. The wind was so strong I could barely keep the door open long enough to walk out.

The fluffy-looking snow from inside was actually slushy ice beating into my face and eyes. "I can do this," I thought. Once I get inside the coffee shop, I will be fine! Off I go. Walking through the snow that was piled up way above my ankles, walking directly against the wind. I made it to the corner of the street, made a right, and walked one block over to my favorite local coffee shop. It actually sat directly across the street from Tom's Diner, which was the outside shot of the Seinfeld diner!

There it was—the long window on the front of the building with a coffee bar perfectly perched to view passersby. I inhaled the cold air with excitement and started toward the door. Locked. No open sign lit. Word was the entire street had lost power due to the storm. I stood there for a moment with the wind whipping around me. For some reason that was the moment I knew my time in New York was over.

Sometimes things aren't as sparkly as they seem, and as sparkly as some moments were, there were moments of feeling lost as well. The coffee shop being closed felt the same as the way confetti looks on the floor on January first after a New Year's Eve celebration. I knew it was time to clean up from a beautiful time in my life, and move on to a new year and a new adventure. It was time for me, again, to trust the magic of new beginnings.

After a year of taking things slow and dabling in things I found interesting: writing, social media marketing, influence, and design, I started my own business as a creative outlet. Erica Lambert Lifestyle was born. From a little baby blog, I have now created a lifestyle business with all the things I love wrapped up into one place. I talk about life, style, and business. Most topics are fun and upbeat, but I also get emotional with my readers when I feel a need. I also offer a service, Champagne Copywriting, to wedding professionals who wish to be featured in a publication or industry-specific blog. I love that everything has come full circle with my wedding-related aspirations!

As my business was really starting to take off, my sweet baby Leo made his arrival into the world, which was an additional fear and obstacle to overcome, in not getting distracted from other goals I had set in my life. I never knew I would feel this way, but Leo came into my life with the most perfect timing. He truly changed my perspective on all the fears of family and structure I had created in my head. He made me look at things differently, and ultimately created more ambition for myself to fulfill my aspirations in life. I didn't lose myself in motherhood, I am career driven, but also driven to be there for him. I embraced a busy life and made sure to take care of myself and devote time to my passions and career so I could be the best and happiest version of me, for him.

The funny thing about life is that it isn't always what you expect, but if you follow your passions, take opportunities, and allow yourself to love, you will find the sparkle at the end of the tunnel. If I were to avoid what my heart was pulling me toward in my personal life, my sought-after professional opportunities never would have made their way to me. Take this book for example, the pretty irony is not lost on me—and I adore that for me and for you.

You can have it all too, Mama!

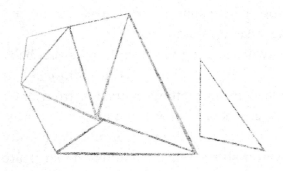

BEING MAMA

Whatever you're doing today, do it with all the confidence of a four-year-old in a superhero t-shirt.

-Author Unknown

Forever Mama

Section 3

Featuring:
Charleyne Oulton
Sarah MacElroy
Samantha Amaraegbu
Sasha Rose

Forgiving
Over-tired
Rude awakening
Ever-changing
Victory/Venture
Entertainment
Relentless

Being a forever mama is being a woman who has the ability to love unconditionally, forever. Children have the power to bring us to our knees with laughter and also, with tears. Motherhood is the greatest, most thrilling and terrifying roller coaster you will ever ride, but you will never want to get off. These women are here to share their journey in an ever-changing world and how to be the constant for their littles.

Robert Munsch had it right with the words, *"I'll love you forever, I'll like you for always, as long as I'm living my baby you'll be."* These are the truest words to remind us that through the giggles and the fighting, through birth and through loss, through the cuddles and boundary testing, you will always be their mama.

For the mamas who have lost a child, before or after birth, you are not alone.

For the mamas crying in the shower so no one sees your sadness, you are not alone. For the mamas snuggling their babies and reading a story, you are not alone.

We are one big community with one big thing in common, we are raising the future population! We can lean on one another when times are hard, and should share our stories of triumph and humor to brighten another mama's day. So go ahead, mama, love those littles with all your might and please, write down those funny things your child(ren) says, get that funny dance on video, talk through your disagreements, be a little less strict on them as they grow. Remember that YOU are their constant, YOU are their mama, forever. There will never be another YOU in their eyes.

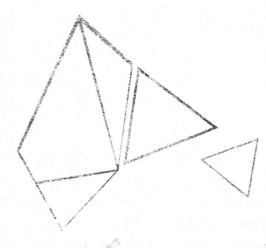

BEING MAMA

My son started school midway through the year. All the kids were playing together when he showed up, and he stood to the side and watched. Another child asked him to play, and my heart burst. I later met that child's mom and told her of her son's kindness. "I'm so glad," she said. "We try to teach him to never let another child sit by themselves or play alone."
In a world where you can be any-thing, be that mom.

@thescarymommy

Chapter Nine

Beginning Again

"Learn to trust your intuition; it is possible to love someone and leave them."

Charleyne Oulton

www.coachcharleybrown.com

ig: @coach.charley.brown | #coachcharleybrown
fb: @coachcharleybrown
goodreads: charleyne oulton
Portraiture by Katie Jean Photography, Mill Bay BC

Charleyne Oulton

Charleyne Oulton, "Coach Charley Brown," is a confident, happy, and divorced mom of three teenagers who lives on beautiful Vancouver Island, BC. She is genuine, experienced, and passionate about creating and maintaining a life full of peace and joy. She is also an appreciated health and wellness coach with It Works Global.

She is a multi-time award winning co-author with Golden Brick Road Publishing House and has been published in: *On Her Plate, Her Art of Surrender, Dear Time, Are You on My Side?*, and the original *You've Got This Mama, Too*. She is also writing in upcoming books to be published in 2020: *She's No Longer Silent,* and *Lighting The North*. Charleyne is a well-known photographer, and a Reservist in the Royal Canadian Navy; she wears many hats. Even through the busy and beautiful chaos of raising a family and adjusting to life after divorce, she loves life and is passionate about encouraging others to thrive.

"The Bhagavad Gita—that ancient Indian Yogic text—says that it is better to live your own destiny imperfectly than to live an imitation of somebody else's life with perfection."
-Elizabeth Gilbert

remember the day my mom and dad sat my older brothers and I down to tell us they were getting a divorce. Even though I was just a young girl, six years old, I can remember parts of this conversation like it was yesterday. I can remember feeling itchy from the coarse fabric of our 1980s couch touching my arm. The tears rolling down my mother's face. The heart-breaking look in my father's eyes, and giving him the longest hug before he walked out our front door. One of my brothers slammed his bedroom door, and the other was very silent. The horrible feeling that this must somehow be MY fault. I also remember blaming my now step-mom for the end of my parents' marriage. I could not have been more wrong. She was not the reason my parents parted. However, I was just a child then and that was my truth. I think this position is common when children are dealing with divorce. Sometimes they blame themselves. Sometimes they blame one of the parents or their new partners. It's simply a coping mechanism. The end of my parents' marriage was the best thing that could have ever happened to them, but it would have been impossible to convince me of this at the time. Now, as an adult, I understand this notion much better. In some situations, divorce is a selfish choice that hurts a family and breaks it apart, but sometimes, it is a choice that is much needed and helps improve everyone's life, health, and wellbeing. What is right for you? This is when you must listen to your gut and really examine your relationship, and be honest with yourself. Is your current relationship building you up? Is it free of belittling, even in the heat of a disagreement? Is your

partner gentle and patient with you, always? Do they celebrate who you truly are inspite of your idiosyncrasies? Learn to trust your intuition. It is possible to love someone and leave them. If you know you need to leave your marriage, or that it is ending, try looking at this choice as a positive start to a new and fulfilling life for you and your family rather than as a failure or act of sin. Sometimes love nourishes your soul and flows freely. Sometimes love hurts and holds you back. Sometimes love is not enough. Once you realize you deserve better, letting go, walking away, and moving on will be the best decision ever, even if it feels terrifying. Be brave enough to start over and to create the life that you have always dreamed of. After all, you can live happily ever after, separately.

Family is family. Family is not determined by marriage, by paperwork, or even by blood. Family is not defined by the people with whom you share DNA. Rather, it is the people in your life who choose to be there. The ones who truly accept you for who you are, regardless of your mistakes or idiosyncrasies. The ones who would do anything to see you smile and who love you no matter what. I am fortunate enough to have a huge and loving family, which includes two mothers and one father. All my parents love me. They have provided for me. They chose me when I was a young child, a rebellious teenager, a teen mother, and now an adult recovering from divorce. I am very lucky.

Parenting is one of the toughest jobs on the planet, requiring endless sacrifice and dedication. To raise successful and strong children, you need to devote countless hours and years to loving, supporting, and teaching them. My second mom chose to love me. She chose my brothers, too. What an amazing woman to choose to devote herself to children whom she did not bear. The words "thank you" are not enough to express my deep gratitude. Nor are the words "I'm sorry" enough to make up for all of the anger and hurtful treatment in the beginning of our relationship.

Our relationship grew stronger year by year because my second mom did not give up on me or my siblings. She became another constant source of love in our world. As Dr Seuss said, "Unless someone like you cares a whole awful lot, nothing is going to get better. It's not."

Surviving Divorce

I never wished divorce for my own children. I still do not wish this chaotic life for them. Yet it is our current reality. They, too, are surviving divorce and all that comes with it. I can honestly say that they are handling the chaos with more grace than I did at their age. Maybe it helps that I can truly empathize with them. I try to acknowledge their feelings daily. To listen to them and pay attention to what they say and how they say it. I have learned to appreciate each and every hug, kiss, drawing, picked flower, or handwritten note. For these are gifts straight from their hearts.

I also try to set a good example daily, whether that is focusing on my children, my own health and mental wellness, or how I talk about their biological father. I make sure the words I use about him are not hurtful or harmful for them to hear. I realize my children love him and are just as much a part of him as they are a part of me; although our marriage has ended, he is still a part of their world.

Dating After Divorce

Dating after divorce is a brand new experience. It is hard. Scary. Awkward. Fun. Exciting. A true mixture of emotions. Dating after divorce is often very hard for children, too. When is it okay to introduce a new partner to your children? This is the million-dollar question, as they say. In my opinion, there is no right answer. My advice is to not rush the process. Allow yourself and your new relationship time to grow. What is right for me and my family might not be what is right for you and for your family. In fact, with every child, family, and situation, it is a different answer.

My children were introduced to my ex-husband's first partner (post-divorce) way too fast (in my opinion). I did not get to be a part of that decision or introduction, and I had to comfort very confused and emotional children when they returned home. I felt such anger and resentment. I remember thinking, *how dare another woman parent my children, and pretend to be their mother, and pretend to live my life?* I struggled with this a lot. Yet as time went on, I realized that there is no stronger bond than the bond between a mother and a child. So I decided to stop second-guessing myself. The only thing I could control were my reactions and my relationship with my children. I learned from this experience that my children needed to be included in any new relationships that I might have and talked about it in advance. In this chapter of life, my children had lots of questions and needed lots of reassurance. They felt much resentment towards my ex-husband's partner. They blamed her for the end of our marriage, much like I did as a young girl.

Isn't It Funny How Your Life Can Come Full Circle?

I poured myself into my children, who were only nine, ten, and twelve years old at the time. Their life was changing drastically in all areas, and I just wanted them to know that some things would never change. I became their constant in a world that now seemed to be spinning out of control. I focused on my relationship with my children, ensuring that we always had and have open communication. We started counselling. I took numerous parenting courses for families who are transitioning, and read countless books and blogs on parenting through divorce. I think it is important to surround yourself with others who are going through the same thing. I reached out to my local health unit, who had recommendations for programs my children and I might benefit from.

People will walk in and out of your life constantly,
but those who truly matter will stay indefinitely.

A Package Deal

When I started dating and met the man I hope to spend my future life with, I was absolutely terrified to introduce him to my children. Thoughts and anxieties spiraled through my head. *What if our relationship does not last, and my children get hurt? What if his family cannot accept me and my divorce? What if my children do not respect him? How will he fit into my chaotic and now broken world?*

I talked to my family and support network a lot about this. It took a long time for me to begin healing from my divorce and put my broken heart back together. I had trust issues and felt anxious to start over. I journaled, prayed, and talked to my kids about dating. I also talked to my new boyfriend a lot and chose to be very honest with him right from hour one. My children are my all, and he needed to respect that I was "a package deal." I came with three kids, baggage, two cats, one dog, an ex-husband, and a whole lot of drama. He reassured me that he would take it slow with my kids, that he felt honored to meet them, and was ready to meet them. We talked about our short-term and long-term goals and found that we had a lot in common. I talked to my ex-husband about this as well, and I decided to introduce our children during a family dinner so they would have lots of support from extended family during this introduction. It was a more casual meeting this way. Nobody felt any pressure (except my boyfriend, I'm sure). What a brave man he was, to come over for Christmas dinner on

Christmas Day to a house full of extended family. In one swoop, he met my mother, her boyfriend, my brother and his wife, my children, my aunts on my mother's side, and one of my cousins. Just in case that was not enough of an overwhelming welcome for him, I also had some of my best friends over.

Welcome to the family, literally.

His Choice

I will never have the words to capture what I thought and what I felt when I held my children for the first time. Nor will I ever be able to describe what joy I feel in my heart when I watch my children and "now" spouse together. The bond they have is beautiful. He chooses them daily, and they are beginning to grow a deep and genuine love for him. It has not always been easy. Not for him. Not for our children. Not for myself. We have our struggles, and it is still an adjustment even though we have been together for twenty-three months. Choosing to become a parent to someone else's children is a big decision. I am not a step-mother, but I do love a man who has chosen to love my children as his own. He joined our chaos without hesitation, and as an outsider. My children were nine, ten, and twelve years old when he met them, ages that are known to be quite impressionable. My children and I have many years of memories and experiences of which he is simply not a part. We encourage the children to talk about these memories freely and to acknowledge that there were some great times before he joined our family. We have had to reassure our children on numerous occasions that he is not trying to replace their biological father and that their dad is always their dad, no matter what; my now spouse is here to join our family and love them as well. I am so thankful for his love and support. He is a good role model, provider, and friend to my children. The bond he has with each of my children is unique. One child calls him

"Dadda" occasionally, the other child calls him by his name, and the third goes back and forth between his first name and "Dad." We have put zero pressure on the children. It's their choice. What will be, will be. We have house rules we enforce and all obey. I choose to allow him to co-parent with me. My children respond well to this. I think they are thriving and responding so well to the consistent love and care they receive

in their lives from their whole support network. That's the thing about co-parenting, and parenting after divorce. The structure and discipline, routine, and love needs to stay constant; otherwise we as adults, co-parents, step-parents have to be very flexible. As the children grow into teenagers, who knows what they might choose, where they might reside, or what issues we might encounter. But I know in my heart that my children will continue to be successful because they are surrounded by people who love and respect them.

The D Word

I never liked the D word (divorce); it always seemed like an ugly word to me. And here I am, a thirty-two-year-old woman with this title. It's not what I would have chosen for myself, but ironically it was the best thing that ever happened to me. This massive life change forced me to put on my big girl panties and become independent for the first time as an adult. I was a teen mom and was with the same man since I was sixteen years old. I never had the chance to be alone or truly discover who I was as a woman outside of being someone's wife or a mother.

Change is hard; it challenged me and terrified me immensely. Who am I? How do I want our normal day-to-day life to unfold? What do I want to do with my life? Where will I live? How will I provide for my family? What will my friends and family think? I learned that I needed to become comfortable with being uncomfortable. Divorce is an uncomfortable process. Change can feel terrifying. Being courageous for yourself is not always the easy choice.

Doing what is right for you can sometimes feel impossible and unattainable. But your ultimate happiness is worth fighting for, and so is your joy. Joy is hope. Joy is always within you.

Today is a good day to start walking away from anyone or anything that causes you more angst than joy.

So, dear, take a leap of faith, have patience, and get out there! Get to know yourself and other people. Be boldly vivacious. Live freely and fiercely. Try new things—you are not who you once were, in or before your last relationship. You have evolved, your intentions and dreams have expanded even if you haven't fully realized them. Your soul has grown and is waiting to be heard, to be loved, to be seen, to *give* you all the possibilities and talents that lie within you to live your best life. Raise your standards and re-evaluate what you are looking for in your life. Take your time, have casual dates with different types of people. Relax, let loose, have fun, and keep it light. It could take time to learn how to communicate, flirt, and get to know someone again. Be honest with yourself and with them. I love meeting new people, but I can admit that I am cautious and tend to be reserved in the beginning of a friendship. I have learned to embrace and enjoy those little butterflies, and I am sure to acknowledge and recognize any emotions that arise.

You will learn a lot about yourself as you start to date after a breakup. My only advice is to date someone who makes you feel confident, happy, and truly enjoys your company.

Try not to compete or compare, but rather learn to embrace the current moment. Life is a gift, and being able to share it with another person is a true blessing.

Much Love,
Charleyne
#coachcharleybrown

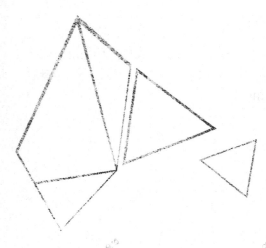

BEING MAMA

Your kids don't need a perfect mom. They need a happy one.

-Author Unknown

Chapter Ten

Every Child is a Lesson

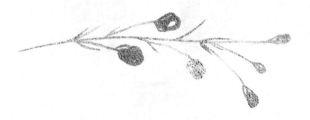

"We must learn to accept and celebrate the children we have for who they are, to walk alongside them on their journey even when it goes along a path we would have never chosen for them."

Sarah MacElroy

www.thewildbrand.com | www.motherofwildthings.com

ig: @Mother_of_Wildthings

Sarah MacElroy

Motherhood was not something Sarah aspired to; she enjoyed traveling and avoiding growing up for as long as she could. After a whirlwind romance and surprise pregnancy, motherhood gave her life a higher purpose. Sarah is currently expecting her fourth child and she is wife to a disabled Army Veteran, Drew. She balances work and family by making sure they are as intertwined as possible. Together she and her husband have built a clothing brand, The Wild Brand, from the ground up. They design and manufacture handcrafted apparel for the whole family in Dallas, Texas. She enjoys homeschooling her sons, and writing about tackling anxiety on her blog, *Mother of Wildthings.* Sarah's debut children's book, *Leaping Lumberjacks* is due to be released in 2021.

As adults, we sometimes become disillusioned when life doesn't turn out exactly as we had planned, as parents, we face this same issue. I am guilty of what my husband calls *Paris syndrome,* I imagine how events will unfold, or experiences will be, I overthink, over analyze, and I set myself up for disappointment time and time again when expectation doesn't live up to reality. After living overseas for about a year, we finally decided to make the (what should have been) a seven-hour drive from our home outside of Nuremberg, to Paris. I had dreamed of traveling to Paris since I was a young girl, and I still held onto some fantastical ideas about how it would be even as an adult. I imagined Paris would be a mecca of nothing but posh, sophisticated, Channel clad women, but everywhere we went it was just heaps of tourists in overalls and air so thick you practically needed to chew it (no offense to the overall-wearing people of the world). Our road trip started with numerous road closures, detours, and ended up taking closer to twelve hours. There was an ozone alert, and the government put out a request that no one drive unless absolutely necessary, but cars and busses still clogged every roadway bringing traffic to a crawl. We eventually arrived and settled into being tourists, but even as we drank *Perrier Jouet* by the Eiffel Tower and wandered the grounds of Versailles, I am ashamed to admit this, I still complained! My imagination had gotten the best of me, and reality left me disenchanted. I did eventually snap out of my funk and enjoyed the remainder of our trip, but these manufactured expectations forever marred part of this wonderful vacation. I am guilty of doing this whenever we plan a vacation; I imagine serene settings, Crate and Barrel perfect rooms, and how perfect everything will be. Reality check: I have three children, age six and under, and *nothing* is ever truly relaxing unless my children are asleep. Optimism is a trait to nurture and cherish, however, unbridled, wishful, or "magical thinking" as my father calls it will lead you to feel disappointed when your expectations do not align with the world around you.

We are a culture that has become obsessed with a picture-perfect, filtered, and distorted existence. It, however, does not exist. Being discontented with one's family or situation is a tale as old as time, i.e., the Prodigal Son parable. Theodore Roosevelt once said, "comparison is the thief of joy," and at some stage of this parenting journey, we must make the decision to allow our children to be who they are intended to be, and be accepting and okay with that. I don't mean to make all of this sound so easy. It can be exceedingly painful to let go of the expectations we have created for our children's lives as they differentiate and become individuals. As an eighties baby, my mother lived for dressing us up in matching Laura Ashley outfits. She was so very proud of my brother and I, and wanted everyone to know she was our mother. That was all well and good when I was four; however, I began making it clear that I didn't like the dresses. I used to twist the buttons off my dresses (while wearing them out), and I was even known to toss my shoes out of a car window when I didn't feel like being a little dress-up doll. This was the first time I truly began exercising my independence, a little foreshadowing for what the future would hold. I grew into a very defiant and strong-willed person, (much to my parents and now husband's ire) that I still am today. Now, this independence will serve children well in adulthood, but we seem to want to squash this character trait in them to make things easier for us. It is our desire as adults to save our children from suffering that I believe pushes us to act in a way that can stifle their differentiation and independence. Some parents have rules about appearances, like *no purple hair under this roof* or *no son of mine will pierce his ears*, but these simple acts of youthful rebellion have no real long-term consequences, other than maybe some stained towels and possibly an ear infection if not done hygienically. My suggestion is not to change your core values or abandon all principles, but to remember being young and impetuous; all the angst and faux romance that swirls all around you as a teenager, the situations you magnify in your mind (i.e. every situation ever). Perhaps you were never impetuous, and you were always cautious and calculated, and you just cannot understand your child. Try. Strive to understand what pushes them, what they love, who they want to be. Find common ground of any kind. My parents and I had seemingly nothing in common, but my dad made an effort to understand why I liked heavy metal music. He was into The Beatles, Jethro Tull, and The Who, he and my mother spent their evenings attending the symphony; seemingly an alternate universe from the European death metal and other music I enjoyed. My father tried to bridge the gap, he would print out lyrics he couldn't understand, and we would spend hours debating their meanings, and occasionally he would venture to concerts with me too. It was not something he ever thought he would do nor enjoy, and truthfully my father never really came to like the music, but he made an effort and ended up forging a bond and creating memories with me that I will carry forever.

We must learn to accept and celebrate the children we have for who they are, to walk alongside them on their journey even when it goes along a path we would have never chosen for them. My parents never ever anticipated that my life would involve some of the things it did, that I would run off with bands as a teenager, tattoo my entire back, or marry a bigamist biker (that is a story for another book)—none of that is something you typically dream your precious child will aspire to do someday. My parents loved me unconditionally and accepted me back every time, without fail, when I ran off and made wild decisions or did things they didn't understand. When their friends and other family members told them the best thing to do was let me go or cut me off, they persisted. Children need love especially when they seem to not deserve it.[1] My parents never condoned my wild behavior or supported it in any way. I had cars taken away and sold, my finances cut back to only the necessities and many, many pamphlets left for me about making good choices. They prayed with me, for me, and always let me know I was their child no matter what, that there wasn't anything I could ever do that would make them stop loving me. I walked a road that my parents could never have conjured up in their worst nightmares. For years I tried to distance myself from my family because I thought my burdens were too painful for them to bear. We must remember that children worry as we do, and most children never want to let their parents down, although their behavior or actions may seem contrary to this. When I was a freshman in college, my father was just three years removed from having cancer and coming so incredibly close to dying. I watched him wither as he accepted his inevitable fate, while simultaneously watching my mother try to keep it all together and never lose hope. During this phase of our lives, I began keeping anything difficult or painful to myself because I just knew in my teenage brain that they couldn't possibly handle anything else. As an adult, I now know this is untrue, and the depth of our feelings and love for our children are immeasurable, and that we can handle so much more than we even know. I lived through years of trauma, and I turned to alcoholism and self-destructive behavior to cope. It took me into adulthood to have the strength to open up about

---

1   Katz, L., & Tello, J. (2003). "I love me!" How to nurture self-esteem. Scholastic Parent and Child, 10(6).

all the sexual assault and physical abuse I had silently suffered through, and that day was the biggest epiphany for my parents. My deleterious choices began to make more sense, they now had the *"why"* that had alluded them for so many years. Many children and young adults will shut down when parents pry, and I know this is a precarious place, but never give up. Change your approach or tactics. Even when children seem too old or to not care, remind them how much you love them and how precious they are, even if they roll their eyes or dismiss you, they hear you. I listened to a podcast recently, Homeschooling In Real Life[2], and one of the hosts said something that stuck with me, he said, *"don't call the game at halftime,"* meaning don't give up on your kid before they have fully developed and grown into who they are destined to be. Don't assume that the future is written in stone; we all have the capacity to adapt. My metamorphosis took almost thirteen long years, and as trite as it sounds, I appreciate all the pain I endured. No one ever expected me to turn into a Christian homeschooling mother of three, but lo and behold, here I am. I am here because I was given so much grace by my parents. I was reminded that there wasn't anything I could do or go through that would make them stop loving me. I know that not every child is given this kind of unconditional love, and in all honesty, I didn't understand this as I was growing up. Can you imagine how much hurt would cease to exist if we all loved our children this way? If we clearly said I love you as you are, for who you are, no matter what. The venerable Mr. Rogers said: "Love isn't a state of perfect caring. It is an active noun like

---

2   Fletcher, Kendra and Andy, hosts. "The Disappointed Parent." Homeschooling in Real Life, 24 July 2019.
https://ultimateradioshow.com/disappointed-parent-2/

struggle. To love someone is to strive to accept that person exactly the way he or she is, right here and now."[3]

We must lovingly push our children to reach their full potential and be a positive force in their life. If you are not the one influencing your child's choices, believe me, good or bad, someone else will. We must push their boundaries positively and encouragingly to promote healthy and well-adjusted development, and simultaneously not infringe on their individuality. I know this sounds flaky at first glance, but we must remember that our children's brains won't fully develop until they are twenty-five[4], so they are going to do some silly things and make bad choices. We are in charge of deciding when it is time to move past pacifiers and bottles, to learn to swim or ride a bike, but we must also be in charge of knowing which of our children's boundaries not to push. Parenting is complicated, and we must navigate the seasons of our children's growth and development, learning when to push and when to back away and just let them be. As parents, we want to prevent our children from experiencing pain and suffering, but unfortunately, this isn't a realistic long-term goal. We can endeavor to protect our babies and toddlers from the dangers in our homes, we buy light socket plugs, we lock up dangerous chemicals, and we warn of stranger danger, but at some point, so much earlier than any of us is indeed ready to accept, we have to allow them to be independent of us. We can't make decisions for our children forever, and much of this power struggle that occurs between strong-willed children and their parents is because we as parents are expecting our children to be like us, to make choices the way we do, to be who we think they should be. Where we derive these expectations from has much to do with

---

3   Rogers, Fred. 2014. *The World According to Mister Rogers: Important Things to Remember.* New York: Hachette Books.

4   Katz, L., & Tello, J. (2003). "I love me!" How to nurture self-esteem. Scholastic Parent and Child, 10(6).

our past and baggage—good and bad that we have from our own upbringing. Children pick up on their parent's subconscious tendencies—maybe you don't even realize some of the things you say about yourself, but I bet your spouse or partner and your children do. As adults, so many of us walk around with wounds from our pasts, some gaping and still raw, others buried a little deeper. What we put out into the world, intentionally or unintentionally, will be radiated at our children. Anger, substance abuse, anxiety, depression, vulgarity, infidelity—these are heavy burdens for any adult to bear, but unbearable for children. Our children can be a mirror into ourselves that we may not want to look into. We must make amends with the past, and accept ourselves as we are right now, thus enabling ourselves to be unburdened in our interactions. We must strive to find contentment within ourselves and in our lives. The examples we live by speak so much louder than the words we say to our children. We may tell our children they are beautiful, but what are we saying about ourselves? We may advise them to respect others, but fail to realize that we fall short of that regularly. It is these discrepancies that children pick up on when we preach to be polite, but shout at and give the finger to other drivers or gossip about our neighbors. I occasionally sit back and watch my two youngest sons pretend-play on the phone or like they're driving, and sometimes I don't like what I see, but they are merely behaving *just like mommy or daddy.* We should expose our kids to both our fragility and humanity as well as our strength, but we tiptoe a very complicated line between being fallible and trying to be perfect because we think that's what our children need to see. We all need more empathy and more grace. Give grace to others freely, instill in your children that we are not our mistakes, we are all worthy of redemption, and it is our job to remind our children of this throughout their lifetime. Remember, at the end of your days, the relationship you have with your child is more important than anything they have ever broken in your home, more important than being a cheerleader or football player, more important than a bad grade, failed class, or momentary bad choice.

It is never too late to make a change; all you must do is decide you want something to be different and make the change. If you and your spouse argue in front of your kids and you don't want to do that anymore? Make a change. If you are comparing your children's aptitudes to one another and not realizing you may be unwittingly causing a sibling rivalry, make a change. Every day we make countless choices and if you don't like how things went yesterday, then change them. If you don't like the parenting style you have settled into, change it. **We are only stuck if we give up.** We long to connect with others, and the most fundamental of these connections is with the people who raise us into adulthood, be they parents, grandparents, foster parents, or whoever undertakes the responsibility of loving a child. Knowing that we are loved and accepted is central for having a happy and well-adjusted life. We will face many challenges throughout the parenting life cycle, from a birth that doesn't go as planned to adjusting to a physical or medical issue we never anticipated, or an adolescent with an attitude problem; this wheel keeps moving on into adulthood, it is not just toddlers and adolescents that will be making us scratch our heads and wonder *why?* Love, unconditional love is what we crave; to be accepted as we are and for who we are is what we need. Every child is a gift, a lesson; embrace and accept the child you have and the journey that brought you to where you are today.

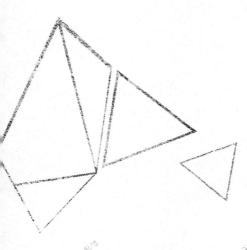

BEING MAMA

Son: Mommy, your hair is weird!
Me: Yeah, I colored it! It's a different color now.
Son: (Frowns) Mommy, can you make your hair go away? I don't like the color.

-Jordie, age 4

Chapter 11

Babies Shouldn't Have Babies

"Don't ever let anyone tell you that you cannot make it, not even yourself."

Samantha Amaraegbu

www.maisonduru.life | www.theglowup.ca

ig: @x0xsamx0x

Samantha Amaraegbu

Samantha Amaraegbu is a paralegal and aspiring author who currently lives in Québec, Canada. While finding her way through school, work, and being a mom, she never gave up on her dreams. Samantha works in the legal field, but is always exploring new and challenging growth opportunities in different fields. With a variety of projects up her sleeve, Samantha will see them to fruition no matter what. Inspired and motivated by her child, Samantha is a mama who is driven, unstoppable, and relentless in pursuit of her dreams.

"I didn't plan on being a single mom, but you have to deal with the cards you are dealt the best way you can."
-Tichina Arnold

1:00 a.m.
Me: "Babe, I think something is wrong . . ."
Him: "What's wrong?"
Me: "I keep waking up in the middle of the
night to pee; I never do that.
And my belly keeps moving and it's not gas.
I think I'm pregnant."

This is where my story began. In the early morning of a cold, chilly November day, an eighteen-year-old college student discovered she was pregnant and going to have a baby.

How was I going to tell my parents? What is life going to be like? A baby? Not a teddy bear, not a toy, not a car, not a laptop, but a human being is inside me. Wait. The baby has a heartbeat, beautiful tiny hands, and feet. The baby continues to grow within me. No matter what, I am going to keep this baby. Yes. It's my responsibility and I will make it.

My name is Samantha Amaraegbu. I am the youngest daughter in a family of four kids. Even though I have a younger brother, for some odd reason, I am still considered the baby (. . . and I was having a baby). Digesting the pill that the youngest girl in the family is having a child was not easy. I had it out for me. At one point, it seemed that everyone was against me. I heard it all—the insults, derogatory comments, the apparent shame I brought to my family. One expression really stuck with me: "Babies should not have babies." (Mind you, I was eighteen years old, not twelve.) I still get these questions today. "How are you doing it all? How do you manage everything—work, school, and your daughter?" To avoid any lectures or unsolicited advice, I usually tell people, "Oh it's okay, it's not that hard, I'm making it happen." If you really want to know, though, here goes the raw truth and nothing but the truth.

Hey teen mama, single mama, you can do this!

The day finally arrived. On July 5, 2013, my beautiful baby was born. A beautiful girl came into this world, eyes wide open. I became a mom at eighteen years old. The first day was hard. My baby wasn't with me. There was a complication in which the umbilical cord was around her neck. She stayed the night in the Neonatal Intensive Care Unit (NICU). Thankfully, it wasn't a long stay, and we were able to go home the next day.

Breastfeeding (which, by the way, was not all unicorns and rainbows the first couple times) was an overall hurtful experience. Who would have thought that one's breast could be so full that a mere arm movement can make you cry? It took me a while to get used to it, but a warm rag at these moments became my best friend. No one, and I mean no one, ever told me that breastfeeding would be painful. Another experience I lived through was the infamous stitches. Yeah. Amazing, right? Wrong—one forgets how to pee or even how to shower.

I got discharged from the hospital on a Monday. It was a beautiful, hot, summer day. Here is where the challenges began. I wasn't living with my daughter's dad at the time. As a matter a fact, I never did. I often wondered whether things would be different had we lived together. Would I still be with him? Would he be more involved in my daughter's life? Would I be less impatient and more understanding?

We started off as a great couple, although my family never met him until my pregnancy. We were happy. After the baby was born, things got a little shaky. The stress of not being together twenty-four hours a day, seven days a week was draining. The build-up of feelings, of not being understood, the lack of help and presence took its toll on us and our relationship. I'm sure I am not alone. We all picture this beautiful perfection for our lives and the lives of our children, but life rarely goes according to plan.

Things hit rock bottom, or so I thought. Our relationship was stormy every day. Thundershowers were calmer than we were. The violence, verbal abuse, physical abuse—it felt scary, toxic, and never-ending.

He was a smoker. All I wanted from him was to stop smoking when the baby was around and to set boundaries with his friends to do the same; if not, then at least to go outside to smoke. Let's just say that he did not take that well. Within seconds, my back was pinned to the wall and I was being shaken. Our baby had just fallen asleep. I couldn't scream or she would wake up, and putting her back to sleep would be another task. I fought back.

Well, I tried to. Hitting his chest and trying to kick him off me, only for him to laugh at me, take me by the throat, and fling my body to the other side of the room. I was paralyzed with shock. I couldn't believe it. I was scared; not for myself, but for my daughter. I had to leave her there overnight because it was really late and it was her christening the next day. We had mutually arranged for her to stay with him overnight so that I could finish the last-minute preparations without any "disturbance." My heart ached with pain, sadness, and worry. I was embarrassed. Now that I think of it, this is the first time I am sharing this incident. I knew, and I still know, if he is ever around her, that he will never hurt his own flesh and blood; however, as a mother, I feared for her well-being, for both of our well-being.

As the usual toxic relationship goes, the sweet talking, the apologies, and the false reassurances took place before I even got home. We were on the phone talking, him singing apologetic words in my ear, convincing me that everything will be alright and that it will never happen again. That is, until what I define as "the eye opener."

It was Thanksgiving. I went to the salon to get my hair styled because we had family coming over. I brought my daughter with me. She was going to spend some time with her father and his family during the day, and then spend some time with my family later that evening. In the days leading up to Thanksgiving weekend, her father and I had been arguing constantly. We both thought that we would be getting married at some point; at least, that's how it had felt. I still had the rings he gifted me on my birthday. Although they were not engagement rings, they still represented a promise we made to one another.

That same Thanksgiving evening, I gave the rings back to him and told him we needed some time to really think about our futures. He put our daughter in her stroller and left her by the door. I was getting her bags ready when he turned me around and pushed me onto his bed. He jumped on me and punched me repeatedly in my stomach. It felt like the air was literally being punched out of me; I screamed and I kicked, calling for help, yet nobody heard my cries. He then continued to assault me by choking me. My eyes were tearing. I couldn't really breathe, and I kept thinking, *am I going to die?* He pulled my pants off and raped me, and that is when his mother walked in, screaming about what was going on. Startled and not expecting anyone to walk in on him, he jumped right off me. I took that opportunity to grab my clothes and my stuff and get out. But before I knew it, he was behind me again. He had a pair of sharp scissors and attacked me with them. I managed to get away and finally left the building, but then his mother was now chasing me. The police were called by a passer-by on the street, and that is how my Thanksgiving ended.

This incident brought on other unpleasant events, such as him stalking me and eventually assaulting me again, spitting on me, attempting to light my jacket on fire, and breaking my glasses. All in one day. This was the end for me. I guess for him as well. Something had to change, so I chose to end the relationship. Here I found my new reality—I was a nineteen-year-old single mother.

After serving time in prison, he moved to another city. I still get calls once in a while, and I encourage my daughter to speak with him and build a relationship with him because regardless of what he did to me and our tumultuous history, he is still her father.

My daughter often has episodes of sudden sadness and mourning, and she misses him. These moments are something every single mother and father must go through. These moments of profound sadness and mourning are something I still do not have a solution to, and these are the moments I still struggle with. How do I answer her questions? Should I ignore them? One day I will know exactly what to do in these situations. But for now, I am doing my best to ensure that she is happy and does not feel alone.

Being a Mama at the tender age of eighteen is also a financial burden. I was not given maternity leave, so I had to look for work as soon as I recovered postnatally. Most young mothers have to go through this. We do not have the luxury to stay home with our bundle of joy for a year. We don't have an income. We have no choice but to enroll our child(ren) in daycare (yes, this is an additional expense) at the earliest age possible. In my case, I had to put my daughter in daycare when she was six months old. My days would start at 6:00 a.m. and end at 10:00 p.m., on a good day. Finding a reasonable and suitable job was the biggest issue we faced. For instance, the companies always hiring are call center jobs; the hours you are most likely to be hired for from the get-go are 4:00 p.m. to midnight, and there is a high probability of working on the weekends. NEXT! You get a minimum wage job and, well, the money you earn is not enough. So here comes the stress, the depression. The feeling of not being able to financially provide for your baby is extremely discouraging.

But, Mama, here is where it gets beautiful. You are strong. You are doing more than the best you can. You are doing fine. I must admit, I never heard these words before, and you may not have either. But it's okay. During my training at one of my previous jobs, my instructor told the group, *"life is like a river, and right now your boat may seem as though it is stuck, but you will soon keep rowing, since the river never ends."* Thank you, Andrew (if ever you read this book)—these words motivated me every time I felt like giving up.

I wanted a better life for myself, for my baby girl. Working these odd jobs was not fun; I could barely earn enough to make ends meet. I decided then that it was time to go back to school. To be fair, I always told myself that I would go back to school, but juggling a baby, school, and work is extremely hard. Let's add taking care of yourself into this mix—something so important, but extremely neglected.

I began a three-year college program in paralegal studies and finally finished the program in 2018. Let me tell you, before I was even able to finish my college program, I was already being ambushed with questions about going to university. Last year was my hardest year. Anxiety, depression, and feeling lost were basically who I became. It consumed me, but I overcame it.

I will go to university on my own timing. Even today, people will approach me and tell me all sorts of things—anything from "well-meaning" but unsolicited advice, to plain unconstructive criticism. I take it in one ear and release it out the other. This is my life, and I am in control.

Young Mamas and young single Mamas, your life has not ended. Your life is not ruined. Your life is just beginning. You will overcome every obstacle you face. You will be successful in everything and anything you put your mind to do. People will talk. That is okay because they will do so regardless of your situation. You will want to give up, you will feel lost, and that is completely normal. Do not give up. You may not achieve your goals right away, but fight and push through despite the fear, despite the odds, and you will get there.

Here is something people tend to forget: Everybody struggles, be it financially or emotionally, be it with a child or without a child, be it single or in a relationship. Everyone hits a bump in the road. The important part is to remember to keep driving. Do not fear, do not worry that your child may not achieve anything because you are doing this alone. They will. They will be bigger than you ever imagined. They will be brighter than the sun. They will shine brighter than a diamond. Why, you may ask? Because you are, forever, their Mama.

Chapter 12

My Beautiful Blue-Eyed Rainbow

*"You will forever be my reason to wake in the
morning, and attempt to rest at night."*

Sasha Rose

ig: @sasharose_4 | @theroseregrowth
fb: @sasharose4

Sasha Rose

Sasha Rose is a woman with big ideas and dreams. She learned from her mother and two sisters that when you have an idea, you put it into action and see it through. Sasha is a budding entrepreneur, with her most recent venture being Oneida Bistro (located South of Ottawa, ON).

Sasha has always wanted to be a mother, and has now been gifted with the ever challenging and rewarding title of mama to her two daughters. She hopes to find a way to make a small difference in this world for her girls to grow up safe and confident.

Sasha is a spiritual woman and an avid animal and outdoor lover. She strives for the life she has always wanted; to own a hobby farm with her family. Sasha is currently working toward her 200-hour yoga teacher certification to heal herself and others. Sasha comes from a mixed background including Scottish, English, and French-Canadian on her mother's side, and Chinese and First Nations-Canadian on her father's side.

ecoming a mother has been the biggest change in my life. I have become one who can run on sheer love when I am sleep deprived. I have become crazier than ever before when my children are defiant and testing boundaries. I am working on becoming the strongest version of myself because I am their example to look up to, I must protect myself in order to protect them.

I am the mother to two stunning and funny daughters, as well as a grieving mother to two babies who I never had the pleasure of holding, kissing, or naming. Here is a peek into my journey into motherhood.

I have always wanted to be a mother, and I always dreamt of starting my family in my early twenties so that I could be done having children and onto raising wonderful humans by age thirty.

When I found out I was pregnant for the first time, it was not planned, especially since the father and I were on again, off again the year prior. There hadn't even been a discussion of being together again, let alone having a child! I accepted the little, growing baby very quickly because of my desire to be a mama—I felt I was going to be okay. The father and I moved in together, well, because I was pregnant. So it made sense, I suppose. Maybe because I didn't want to do it alone? Maybe because I didn't want to be judged?

I went through my routine appointments, scans, and blood tests that are to be expected in early pregnancy with flying colors, and there were no red flags that anything daunting was to come. I had no morning sickness and I could feel that little peanut growing within—my heart was full.

On New Years Eve the spotting began while singing karaoke at a small gathering and sipping sparkling apple juice; we were celebrating! I tried to relax. I curled up in the large leather recliner and sat quietly for the remainder of the evening. As soon as we got back home we went to the E.R. for a scan, where my doctor met us and quickly broke my heart in two. I had lost the baby. We were devastated. It broke my hope for a family. I then had to tell my friends and family that we had spilled the beans to, that there was no longer a bundle of joy to come. This was just a constant reminder of the heart break. I wondered if I would ever be able to have a child. What did I do wrong? Am I unhealthy? Is it because I drank alcohol while pregnant (unknowingly) before a positive test? Is it because I spent time with my horse or was one of my exercises or hikes too much? My doctor assured me that there was nothing that I had done to cause this loss, but my guilt set in and I analyzed the last two weeks to try to find a reason to give me some closure. I still think of the what-ifs of this lost peanut to this day.

The father and I continued our relationship and decided to try again in the future. I now wanted a child so badly. We moved to a new town, I started two new jobs and he was on unemployment insurance and "searching" for a job. I put that in quotations because sitting in the yard drinking beer is not very efficient job hunting. I found out I was pregnant two months later and was thrilled. This time was different, boy-oh-boy was I ever sick! I actually lost weight in the first five months of pregnancy. Was this a sign that this pregnancy would be healthy? I immediately started my prenatal vitamins and stopped any consumption of alcohol. The only thing I could stomach for the next five months was potatoes, ramen noodles, water, spinach, and strawberries with feta cheese—oh and lemons, I loved lemons!

This time was going to be different, I did not tell a soul I was expecting until the twelve week mark—that magic "safe zone," where you are out of the most threatening time for a spontaneous miscarriage, according to our doctor.

I was working early mornings and late nights and my back began to ache, sleep was difficult to achieve, and my feet were sore. *Is this normal for only four months along?* I was barely showing yet (thanks to my baggy work shirt). I felt the first flutter of this baby the first week of October, it stopped me in my tracks and I smiled. I was going to be a Mama! My heart was full again—the sadness looming from my lost baby was fading to a memory.

Jump ahead to my due date and still no baby. I was huge, ginormous, like I had a planet stuck underneath my shirt. My doctor was concerned for a large baby, so he encouraged me to try to self-induce labor. So I walked the high-school track and climbed the stairs at the school field over and over again, ate spicy food, and did (well, attempted) squat after squat. All of this despite my extreme sciatica, my heart burn, lack of sleep, and my center of gravity being off-kilter! I waddled like a giant penguin and probably sounded like a winded pig. I was determined to avoid induction.

I was now one week overdue, it was about 10:00 p.m. and my cell phone rang. I had just finished doing the cat-cow yoga pose (more cow than cat) to try to get my damn baby to drop! It was my doctor, "how'd you like to get induced tomorrow?" he said. Without hesitation I answered with an exhausted "yes, please!"

I rushed (at snail speed) to make sure my hospital bag was packed . . . of course it was, I had probably checked my list ten times, and repacked and reorganized it twenty times. I tried to get some rest before the big day.

The next morning was full of quiet excitement as I tried to imagine what the next twenty-four hours would hold for me. How fast will the baby arrive? Can I avoid medication and go the natural route? How much is this going to hurt? The only thing that mattered was that I was going to get to hold my rainbow baby for the first time.

What a whirlwind of a day. It started with the induction itself at about 11:00 a.m., which took no more than fifteen minutes. *Hmm . . . okay, that was easy,* I thought to myself. My mother, sisters, boyfriend, and I went for a nice meal a few blocks from the hospital to try to keep my mind off of what was to come. About halfway through my meal I began to get a familiar menstrual like pain in my lower back. *OH MY GOSH, was this it?! It's starting!* I was excited and terrified all at the same time. We headed home and my boyfriend left; I guess he didn't feel the need to hang around and make sure I was okay? Whatever, I had my mama and sisters there, they were my support.

I laid on the couch and requested a heating pad, the cramping was getting worse by the minute. It had gotten to the point where I could no longer get comfortable, and was moaning in discomfort. I asked if we could head to my boyfriend's parents house so I could use their large soaker tub to try to relax. It was about 5:00 p.m. at this point. This was the most intense sensation I had ever felt, the most intense cramps that came and went. I drained the hot water tank because the water was not hot enough, his family was boiling pots of water and the kettle to keep me warm, my entire body was shivering. I also needed, and I mean *needed*, a steaming hot peppermint tea, with a side of ice cold water. Pregnancy causes remarkable, strange, and intense feelings and cravings, for me, labor was even worse! All of a sudden my contractions went from eight to ten minutes apart, to three to five minutes apart, but they only lasted for ten to twenty seconds. I demanded we call our doctor and he said, "but they aren't long enough contractions yet, wait a bit and call me back." *What?! Wait?!* As soon as he hung up the phone, I became sick to my stomach (good thing for the pot that had previously held boiling water beside the bathtub). *"CALL HIM BACK"* I exclaimed. The doctor still was not convinced and then *cramp, POP, whoooooosh* . . . my water broke. It felt like a balloon popping inside me— how bizarre! I tried to get my quivering, beluga-like body out of the tub to dry off so we could leave, my boyfriend just stared at me. "Umm . . . can you hand me my pants?" I stated. I hobbled and contracted the whole way out of the house to the truck and plunked my aching body into the front seat of the lifted truck (on a towel, I didn't want to wreck the seat!). My boyfriend's father drove us to the hospital, he was too scared. We arrived just before 7:00 p.m. and the door was locked. WHAT! I could barely stand. Finally someone came to the door and we got a wheelchair and I was rushed down to maternity where they were waiting for me. I was convinced that I was going to be almost fully dilated and almost ready to go. "Four to five centimeters," the nurse said. I stared at her and thought, *that's it? I have to continue this pain for how much longer?!*

My mother and sister's met us at the hospital. The nurse proceeded to place an I.V. in my left hand, while I tried to lay still. My blood pressure must have been very high because there was blood squirting from my hand onto the floor. The nurse dropped the I.V. set on the floor, and luckily my mother was there and grumbled "ahem," because the nurse was going to pick it up and use it! *Ew.*

I laid on my side and requested cups full of ice chips, dozing off between contractions. My mother was waiting in the room with me, so was my boyfriend (but he stood in silence in the corner), and my sisters walked in. My one sister nervously glanced at me, then glanced at my bright pink toe nails (from a recent pedicure) and said, "awe, at least your nails look pretty." Thanks a lot . . . I know I looked like a sweaty mess. We all laughed, and then another contraction came. My other sister said something along the lines of, "this is great birth control." Again, thanks for the humor, while I am experiencing the worst pain in my life. It didn't take long for me to cave and request the epidural, the pain was just too intense and I was only five to six centimeters dilated. It took at least an hour before the anaesthesiologist arrived to give me the goods, and while having a large needle jabbed a few times between my vertebrae is a horrible sensation, the relief it provided me seemed like magic. He taped the line to my back and I began to relax. My mother came back in the room and she thought I was given a sedative because I was so calm and relaxed, very zen. I informed her it was just because I was pain free!

We all sat up and talked for a bit, then I decided I should try to get some rest since the nurses were back every hour to check my progression.

Here we were, 5:00 a.m., onto hour eighteen of my first-born journey, and I am finally ready to start pushing. I had every expectation that this was going to be easy, that I would be able to birth like my mother. Her doctor told her she was made to have babies, that she had birthing hips. She had five children, all natural, without issue! Well, I have the same hips, so I figured this would be a breeze. So why wasn't this baby budging? Why wouldn't this baby drop? Why couldn't I do this? I was trying my darndest to get that baby out, but with no success. I was hooked up to all the monitors, but I couldn't feel anything because of the epidural. There were two nurses, two student doctors, my boyfriend, my mother, and my doctor. I was on display under harsh fluorescent hospital lights for everyone to see. Bye, bye dignity. My nurses provided zero guidance on when to push, so I was feeling very overwhelmed. The doctor informed me that my baby was stuck in the posterior position, otherwise known as "sunny side up," which means the baby was forward facing and not in the ideal position for birth. My baby was "stuck" on my pelvic bone and was not budging. I pushed for two hours and was exhausted. I was told I needed a c-section to deliver my baby safely. I had not mentally prepared for a cesarean. Surgery was a very scary thought to me, but potentially harming my baby by continuing to push wasn't an option. So I signed the consent form and they rolled me off to the surgical room. There I was, exposed, marked up, swabbed and washed up like a raspberry, hooked up to multiple monitors, shivering under the surgical lights. Multiple doctors and nurses seemed to be dancing around me in preparation, setting up their stations. The anaesthesiologist was fabulous, he was tending to me with little sponges of water to cure my dry mouth, and checking in constantly to make sure I was okay. My boyfriend sat there in fear in a blue cap and gown. I recall the sensation of ice being moved from my chest down my belly to make sure I was numb for the first incision. It was just after 8:00 a.m. and the surgeon began. There was wiggling and jiggling, and the sound of instruments clanging on metal surgical trays. I stared up at the giant, white, round surgical light and could see a bit of my reflection in the silver rim of the lights. *Are those my insides?* I thought to myself. I began to feel faint, so the doctor gave me some more drugs to counteract whatever else he has given me. "You're going to feel some pressure," the surgeon said. Yup, he was right, it was like laying on an exercise ball, everything felt displaced. Three. Two. One. Then he sliced open my womb.

Her first cry was powerful and she wasn't even out of my body yet. The second air hit her, she gasped, took a breath, and announced to the world that she had arrived. They raised her up like Simba from the Lion King, so I could see her over the drape and I thought she was so tiny! They said she was going to be big! She was mine. Tears streamed down my face. My boyfriend got up and got to cut the cord and see her get cleaned off and weighed. He had skin-to-skin contact with her and I got to kiss her forehead. I couldn't hold her because my arms were strapped to the table to keep the I.V. lines secure. They stitched me up, sat me up a little bit, and wheeled me back to the first delivery room. My baby girl was born at 8:18 a.m. People always say the love that rushes over you when your child is born is overwhelming, I did not understand the magnitude of this until that moment arrived. Be present in that moment, as much as you can be because you will remember it for the rest of your life. Relish in those split second moments of candid laughter and imaginary play as your child grows, at times these moments will feel far and few between. Cherish their messes and forts because they only last so long before you start arguing over who is going to clean up the mess! When they hand you a rock or a weed, show extreme gratitude, for they had you in mind when they thought that item was perfect enough to pick up. You will receive endless sketches, drawings, and cotton ball art, and if you are anything like me, you will have boxes full of it because you can't stand to part with it! Regardless of how you came to be a mama, that little child (or children) were meant to be in your life.

My children excite me, challenge me, test me, and often anger me. I have learned to focus on my breathing in times of high tension. They bring laughter, love, and light into my life. My worries and anxiety since becoming a mama are through the roof, but all I can do is help teach and guide them on how to navigate this crazy world, to be kind, follow your passions, and be strong. I will forever be grateful for my children choosing me to be their mama.

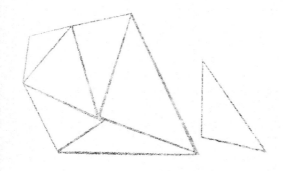

BEING MAMA

You will never know true anxiety, until you're in a bathroom stall with your toddler, pants around your ankles, mid pee, and your kid unlocks the door.

-Author Unknown

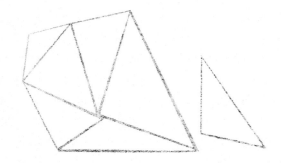

BEING MAMA

In our son's four years of life, he has only slept through the night twice. Which means for the last four years, I've also only slept through the night twice. And those two nights I'm pretty sure I didn't actually sleep through the entire night because I was confused why my child didn't wake like he usually did. I long for the day I can sleep without interruption and to actually feel rested in the morning.

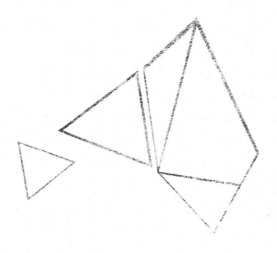

When we snuggle in bed before he falls asleep, we talk often about why he needs to sleep through until morning, and to try to not come and find me in my bed. His answer to me is always something along the lines of "but it makes me sad when you're not in my bed," or "it makes me happy when I come find Mommy!"
I guess I will not be sleeping through the night in my own bed anytime soon.

-Lola T. Small, GBR Author,
Jordie's Mom

Acknowledgments

"I would like to thank my beautiful daughter for teaching me how to see the world through her eyes, and to my mom for showing me what it is to love"

-Deirdre Slattery

"To my children for joining me in the kitchen, my mother, Kathy, for teaching me how to bake cookies, my father, Jeff, for the tradition of Saturday morning pancakes, my mother, Libby, for teaching me the importance of a family dinner, and Jonathan for sharing your traditions."

-Charleyne Oulton

"To my beautiful Mira, my mother, my sister, my aunts, and all my girlfriends. To all the mamas in this book and everywhere in the world. To all women."

-Liz Vardan

"For both my Mom and my son, for teaching me how to be a mother."

-Shannon Figsby

"To Mae Bergin and Lisa Sarker, I wouldn't be where I am without the endless support. You both scraped me off the ground when the pressure of being a mother became too much to bear. You are my soul sisters."

-Habiba Jessica Zaman

"To my grandmother for the life lessons you gave me prior to passing on. To my daughter for choosing me to be her mother; she has given me tremendous purpose. Lastly, to my friend, mentor, and boss, Clara Cohen."

-Jenna Knight

"To Sage; may you always love yourself unconditionally, share your light, and expect miracles. To my husband; Thank you for being strong for our girl and supporting my aspirations. To my family and the women in my life, you are my soul tribe."

-Valerie Steele

"To my husband, Dad, Mom, and brother. Thank you for always believing in my love and passion for writing and motivating me. To my boys, Leo and Fox, thank you for making me a better human being."

-Erica Lambert

"The dedicated team at Golden Brick Road Publishing House richly deserves my praise for another job well done. I thank all of you for your continued support."

-Charleyne Oulton

"To my mother and father; thank you for never giving up on your wild child."

-Sarah MacElroy

"A special thank you to my beautiful daughter—without you in my life, I would not have discovered my strength."

-Samantha Amaraegbu

"To my bug, you will forever be my reason to wake in the morning, and attempt to rest at night. I hope that you can always come to me to be your compass, confidante, hard truth, and friend. You are my rainbow baby. Love, your Mom, Mama, Mommy"

-Sasha Rose

GOLDEN BRICK ROAD
PUBLISHING HOUSE

Link arms with us as we pave new paths to a better and more expansive world.

Golden Brick Road Publishing House (GBRPH) is a small, independently initiated boutique press created to provide social-innovation entrepreneurs, experts, and leaders a space in which they can develop their writing skills and content to reach existing audiences as well as new readers.

Serving an ambitious catalogue of books by individual authors, GBRPH also boasts a unique co-author program that capitalizes on the concept of "many hands make light work." GBRPH works with our authors as partners. Thanks to the value, originality, and fresh ideas we provide our readers, GBRPH books are now available in bookstores across North America.

We aim to develop content that effects positive social change while empowering and educating our members to help them strengthen themselves and the services they provide to their clients.

Iconoclastic, ambitious, and set to enable social innovation, GBRPH is helping our writers/partners make cultural change one book at a time.

Inquire today at www.goldenbrickroad.pub